JESUS OF NAZARETH

Borgo Press Books Written or Translated by Frank J. Morlock

Anna Karenina: A Play in Five Acts, by Edmond Guiraud, from the
   Novel by Leo Tolstoy

Anthony: A Play in Five Acts, by Alexandre Dumas, Père

The Children of Captain Grant: A Play in Five Acts, by Jules Verne
   and Adolphe d'Ennery

Crime and Punishment: A Play in Three Acts, by Frank J. Morlock,
   from the Novel by Fyodor Dostoyevsky

Falstaff: A Play in Four Acts, by William Shakespeare, John Den-
   nis, William Kendrick, and Frank J. Morlock

Jesus of Nazareth: A Play in Three Acts, by Paul Demasy

Joan of Arc: A Play in Five Acts, by Charles Desnoyer

The Lily in the Valley: A Play in Five Acts, by Théodore Barrière
   and Arthur de Beauplan, from the Novel by Honoré de Balzac

Michael Strogoff: A Play in Five Acts, by Adolphe d'Ennery and
   Jules Verne

The Mysteries of Paris: A Play in Five Acts, by Prosper Dinaux and
   Eugène Sue

Peau de Chagrin: A Play in Five Acts, by Louis Judicis, from the
   Novel by Honoré de Balzac

A Raw Youth: A Play in Five Acts, by Frank J. Morlock, from the
   Novel by Fyodor Dostoyevsky

Richard Darlington: A Play in Three Acts, by Alexandre Dumas,
   Père

The San Felice: A Play in Five Acts, by Maurice Drack, from the
   Novel by Alexander Dumas, Père

Shylock, the Merchant of Venice: A Play in Three Acts, by Alfred de
   Vigny

The Voyage Through the Impossible: A Play in Three Acts, by Adolphe d'Ennery and Jules Verne

William Shakespeare: A Play in Six Acts, by Ferdinand Dugué

JESUS OF NAZARETH

A PLAY IN THREE ACTS

by

PAUL DEMASY

Translated and Adapted by Frank J. Morlock

THE BORGO PRESS

An Imprint of Wildside Press LLC

MMIX

CONTENTS

DEDICATION

To

JOHN LANGFORD

INTRODUCTION

I am describing this as an adaptation rather than a translation because I've taken more liberties with the text than is my normal practice when translating a play. While the work remains very faithful to the original, I've felt necessary to omit a few lines and include others for clarification purposes. I've also removed or changed a few references that might be taken as racist or anti-Semitic. I do not believe that was the author's intent, so removing this material is like removing a smudge or blemish on a larger work of art. Their presence detracts, their removal enhances. I'm speaking of no more than a half dozen lines. Probably, they would go unnoticed; but given the political circumstances of our times and rising anti-Semitism I've chosen to suppress them. This is not, as with obscenity, something that is merely offensive to some. Racism has political consequences and I do not wish to add even a droplet to that poisoned stream. The political climate a few years ago was calmer and my decision might have been different in those days or in more happy times to come. In any event, the changes were extremely minor.

This drama is almost two plays. Act One is mainly

about John the Baptist. Acts Two and Three are about Jesus and Judas. The personality of Jesus is the linchpin which ties them together. This is a play which may be better in its parts than as a whole. Act One might be performed separately as a play about John the Baptist. All or part of Act One might be omitted from the second play which is about Jesus and Judas. Act Two or Act Three might be played separately as well or individual scenes as separate one act plays. It's a rich banquet which will provide many a feast.

CAST OF CHARACTERS

ELEAZER
NATHAN
CLEOPHAS
SIMON PETER
ANDREW
BARZILAI
A PHARISEE
JESUS
DANIEL
SARAI
NICODEMUS
JOSEPH OF ARIMATHEA
JOHN THE BAPTIST
KANTHERA
CENTURION
FIRST SOLDIER
SECOND SOLDIER
A PUBLICAN
A SOLDIER
A JAILOR
HEROD ANTIPAS
THE EXECUTIONER

JUDAS

CAIAPHAS

ANNAS

PHAROS

JOEL

JOHN

JAMES

LAZARUS

SELOMITH

FIRST LICTOR

SECOND LICTOR

A PHARISEE

ANOTHER PHARISEE

HERODIAS

SALOME

MARY MAGDALENE

MARTHA

VERONICA

JONATHAN

ACT I

SCENE I: THE DESERT

The desert near Jordan. A grotto.

The crowd arrives in groups, men, women, children. Among them, Andrew, Simon, Eleazer, Jonathan, disciples of John.

JONATHAN: They are coming in greater numbers every day.

ELEAZER: They are coming from everywhere. From Moab, from Ephron and even Idumea. And Jerusalem isn't slow to send its children.

JONATHAN: They couldn't come with greater difficulty. Isn't it strange, this fascination with the desert and with the voice which shouts in the desert?

SIMON: Tell me, Jonathan, are there rich men and savants among them?

JONATHAN: See, Simon.

ANDREW: The ones over there are Jews. They are priests and doctors, Pharisees and Sadducees, that Jerusalem is sending to question John. Yesterday, others came. Ah, Simon, new disciple, dear Brother, if you heard the Master call them "Race of Vipers" and "White Sepulchers"! Mantles of hypocrisy.

A MAN: The seer will speak today, Lord?

ANDREW: He will speak if God commands him to speak.

MAN: I have my wife and my son and we made a long journey to hear him and be baptized.

ANDREW: From where are you coming, brother?

MAN: From Nazareth, in Galilee.

ANDREW: Barzilai!

MAN: That's my name! You know me?

ANDREW: And you don't recognize, Andrew, son of Jonas, the fisherman of Capernaeum? And my brother, Simon?

BARZILAI: I recognize you now. And you are coming like us?

ANDREW: We are disciples of the seer. And we baptize like him and by his order. And he directs us to consecrate our lives to repentance because the Messiah is approaching.

BARZILAI: The Messiah is coming!

A MAN: The Messiah is coming?

ANDREW: So says the seer!

THE CROWD: The Messiah! He says the Messiah is going to come. He says the Messiah is going to come. The Son of David! The King who must not die! He is coming. The one who will save us. The exterminator of the Romans. The Day of Israel! Messiah! Messiah!

BARZILAI: Jesus Bar Joseph! The seer is announcing the Messiah is come. Be happy, man! Do you know the sons of Jonas, Simon and Andrew?

JESUS: I know them.

BARZILAI: You will be able to announce the good news, carpenter, to Mary, your mother, and to the brave Joseph who is the best Israelite that I know. Are you coming to get yourself baptized, too?

JESUS: I came for that.

BARZILAI: That's very fine, young man. Tell me, for

indeed you please me a bit. Aren't you yet thinking of marrying a brave woman? I assure you, cousin, that I have not had to repent of being married. Imbecile that I am! Where's my head? Excuse me! I was forgetting that Mary made you a Nazarene! I had lost sight of you for a while. I hadn't taken note of your hair! That good Mary. At least you are not going to trouble her by becoming a disciple of the seer. You owe her a little, cousin!

JESUS: I was hers for thirty years.

BARZILAI: Thirty years! You are already thirty years old. How time passes. It reminds me again—(they pass on)

THE CROWD: Messiah! Messiah! He's come. The Saviour of Israel.

SIMON: But this credulity you smile at contains in its power all the troubles. It's the tree of revolt on which Rome's thunder will fall. Let's keep an eye on these agitators. How they dress, besides, like Tolmai, with wool, or like this one in camel skin. There are as many perils for Jerusalem in the revolt of a leather belt and an unwashed head of hair as in the furor of a self styled enthusiast for the crown and laurels.

THE CROWD: Jehovah! Jehovah! Be propitious to your people! You see our ills. Make health rain! Baptism! Baptism! And let the Messiah rule! Son of David! We implore you! Praise to Jehovah! God of Israel, sole

God! Before whom tremble the idols and the Domina-
tions. Send your Christ, God of Abraham, our father,
God of Jacob, God of David!

SIMON: Shut up, ignorants, wretches!! Don't you know
that Elijah must succeed first, before the Messiah
comes? And when he appears, the prophet vows you
will hear his terrible voice before having seen his face.
Silence! Pray, fast, be charitable if you want God to act.
It's not to the desert that God speaks, and you know
where his temple is. The desert makes you senseless.
Go find reason again, if you ever had any, in Jerusalem,
in the Synagogues. You have priests and doctors. We
are there to instruct you, blind troupe. Fulfill the Law!
And you will shine on the Day of God. Stupids, why do
you come to dispute with the jackals their dwelling
place? What is it that attracts you from the depths of
your small towns, with women and children? What will
of the wisp? A man who howls like a wild beast? A
madman who eats locusts? Or the hope of a little water
on the head or an immersion in the Jordan? But you
have rivers everywhere and all purifications; the misfortune of the weather and the heat of the Sun and the
wrath of Jehovah come where there is an abundance of
lunatics, and legions of possessed! Go away! When Elijah comes we will inform you. We will give you a meeting at the Temple on the day we enthrone the Messiah
over all Israel.

JOHN: (appearing in the doorway of the grotto) Well
then, what have you come seeking here, Pharisee? In

the desert of Jehovah? And if you scorn the eater of locusts, why are you coming to listen to him? Ah, you also felt the suffering, the burning air, the wind of wrath to come. You smell death even in your synagogues, and like a troupe of the blind you seek the company of those possessed by God; you seek health from lunatics, you wait for him to reassure you. Rabble! Hear what the lion of Israel says! "Your incense stinks to me. Your sacrifices and your prayers fall back on the soil like a ball thrown by the weak hand of a child! Tribe of Levi, I had instituted you to be the shepherd of Israel! You have led it to bitter pastures where it only browses to its perdition. I no longer see in Israel anything but Sodom and Gomorrah and forests of idols." Enthrone the Christ! Receive the prophet! Ah! Ah! Ah! You have gold, incense, marble and harps, but your heart is named luxury, your spirit domination, your body sin. Live in sin, your hands smell of death and it's not on your gold incense burner and harps that Jehovah implants the throne of Christ. At the sight of the Messiah, your faces will become like ashes and all your science, doctor, will vanish, just as the green fire of fireflies will be extinguished in the living fire of the day of Truth. Your death is coming and the day of Gehenna, you bandaged mummy, so that you, too, beating your breast with your fist, and failing to look at your rotting soul, you will present yourself at the Jordan, baring your flesh, nourished on vice, the fruits of death and pride, bowing before the gestures of the Eater of Grasshoppers or the most ignorant of his disciples. Be humble, Pharisees, doctors, priests and scientists, you pride of Satan. Return into yourselves and try not to die of terror! If you were to see as I see, you would think: Is this me? This vomit and this malady? Is this me, this worm shriveled on the embers? And if you could see yourself with the eye of the Eternal, with that exacting, meticulous and pitiless eye that nothing obscures, the shadow of the most subtle and delicate cloud, O Pharisee, colossus of pride and self satisfaction, you would collapse, melt like a slug under a pinch of salt, like snow by a burning lens, you would bellow out a sob to move the brass of heaven. But you laugh, saying to yourself, "This man is demented from living amongst the sand and stones, he's taken on the nature of the hyena and vipers, venom has fanged him. He's no longer a man!" You brother, you hear me, I am your brother, miserable and filthy like you, but a miserable one who weeps and a filthy one who blushes. And as for me, Pharisees, and as for me, too, Sadducees, I came to the desert because my eye had ceased to please itself at what made yours delight, and my deafened ear, deafened by your canticles, no longer heard the interior murmur, the bitter psalm of repentance. At that time I tore off the dress which hid my infirmity, the pride of life which blinded me, and all the sensuality of a happy animal. He judged me worthy, he, Jehovah, to hear his word and to understand naked, without the commentary of the Temple. And I am no more than a voice which cries, swelled by the Eternal Word of the Eternal! Prepare the way for him who is going to come and who will baptize, by fire and by spirit those that he finds purified; for him who will be, like you a son of man and of woman, but having abdicated the rags of vain glory and the turban of vanity through which you think to distinguish your humanity from the brute. He's coming, the new David, with neither turban, nor miter, but with an unbearable star blazing in his face, the King, the Judge, before whom all impure flesh liquefies. The God man who knows neither tears, nor laughter. The Messiah of Israel, but who will destroy Israel if he doesn't find it perfect.

THE CROWD: Baptize us! Baptize us! I repent. I abjure my sin. Purify us. Prophet, tell us what we must do!

(Enter a litter born by slaves and an escort of soldiers commanded by Kanthera.)

KANTHERA: Make way! Make way!

ELEAZER: The Herodias.

JONATHAN: The King.

THE CROWD: Baptism! Baptism!

NICODEMUS: He speaks like the prophets.

JOSEPH: My heart leapt to hear him. There's more truth in him than in us. He's got the people inspired.

NICODEMUS: It's not eloquence, it's more than that.

JOSEPH: Nicodemus, he's the word of life and the breath

of God.

KANTHERA: Make way for the Queen!

A MAN: Down with the Herodians!

CROWD: Messiah! The Baptist!

HERODIAS: (appearing) Kanthera, what is it?

KANTHERA: Queen, it's a sort of hairy beast who is preaching and haranguing the people who hear him.

JOHN: Ah, Jezebel, you dare to approach the cave of the Lion! What are you coming here to do, prostitute?

HERODIAS: It's John. I see him at last. Show yourself, Salome, we are going to hear pretty insults! Slaves, lower the litter! (Herodias and Salome get out of the litter) Salome, those there are not Romans.

SALOME: Who are they then?

HERODIAS: Jews; my people and yours!

SALOME: With what an eye this animal looks at us!

JOHN: Israel! Behold your Queen! Herodias! Such is the name of prostitution seated on your litter. Herod Antipas, of the tribe of Edom, the grandson of the Temple sweep, Tetrarch of Galilee, by the grace and the might of Rome. Antipas, the adulterer called them, she and her daughter from Rome; he winked and she left the bed of Philippus for the bed of the brother of Philippus, and she brought her daughter that Rome had educated in luxury, and who knows how to dance in dives to amuse the man from Machaerus, starving for a new lechery. Behold your masters, Israel! Adore them! And behold the Christ that you deserve, the new Ahab, and the new Jezebel. And here, all decked out, people and Pharisees, vice and pride and ignominy that you hide from all except God! Israel, behold yourself revealed to yourself! Here you are unmasked. You think yourself beautiful, Herodias, and what you denominate your beauty is the only book you want and know how to read. But, because learned in this perishable science, painting your wrinkles, perfuming your skin to hide the beast and bestial odor, masking your arse, adorning with diamonds your breasts, and carrying your head high with a golden smile, you have charmed Antipas, who you've dispossessed of his wits, turning him thus away from the Arab girl he married; and thus reigning over the human debris. You await from Rome the title and the tiara of Queen. Do you think to stupefy a standing man the way you've enchanted a man in bed? The man of the desert laughs to see the slut standing on her feet, whose natural posture he knows is to march on her hands and knees, closer to the ground, smelling the odor of mud. And Jehovah who created you for what mysterious and terrible ends, O dancing girl, perfumed corpse, man-trap, and tomb of his strength, O shameless harlot of Israel! Jehovah, when animating you with his thumb, was already looking at the ash heap where your puny bones will be pulverized along with your less corruptible jewels and the myriad of worms feasting on your flesh. Yuck! I prefer the odor of my excrement to the stench of your armpit, the tannery of the bear to the room where you sleep, and the corrosive fire of the mid-day sun to the heat of your breast. You laugh, Herodias, with the little demon at your side? You laugh adulteress, you laugh incestuous one, you laugh murderess? But these are the last days of your laughter, for behold the whirlwind which swallows Machaerus, the fortress of your debauches! And behold the King whose Queen you will no longer be. He lives, understand me? The Son of David, that your fathers were expecting. The days of Antipas are numbered. Tell him that. The Tetrarch will no longer be king. Another at this moment is breathing, amassing in his breath the immortal wrath. I see him, I feel him, I divine him. He's coming, calm and sure, and Machaerus is no more than a ruin haunted by nocturnal carrion. Antipas, a cadaver, his Jezebel, I don't know what I can call her, but on whom the jackal will feast!

HERODIAS: Kanthera, seize him! The Tetrarch will not let me be outraged. The rest of you arrest him!

KANTHERA: This crowd will hurl itself on us. Can't you hear it grumble?

HERODIAS: Let's return.

KANTHERA: The Tetrarch knows him and leaves him

free, fearing a revolt.

HERODIAS: He's provoking it by leaving this man alive! Go on!

KANTHERA: (whispering to her) Hear me.

JOHN: O God, pity on me! I haven't tongue and I haven't breath! Give voice to this Sun, these palms, these mountains! What do you want of me, reed, and what word to utter to move this eyeless, earless and unintelligent people? A strange hunger rages in my belly. To be the lightning and to speak so as to cleave these hard skulls, which knowledge ravishes, and to put blood in these locked hearts! I am ill with your spirit and suffering all the sorrow of childbirth. Horror! Shall I say the word? And do you want me to condemn Israel? (Herodias and her escort have gone) People, hear what Jehovah, the Eternal, has commanded me to tell you. Israel has never known me. Israel is not my people. It nourishes idols in its breast. Israel entrusts itself to the descendants of Abraham, as if I could not make pebbles of the sons of Abraham, stones in which I would find greater docility and true belief! Israel has allowed itself to be saddled and bridled and has allowed foreign cavaliers to ride on my back. For golden oats in mangers of marble, it has given itself over to Kings who blaspheme my name, erecting altars and turpentine trees in all the high places and Pharisees who have blindfolded Israel's eyes and who amuse Israel with peas shaken in a bladder, and because Israel has rejected the cavalier Jehovah, who rode it bareback, without bridal or bit, guiding it only with the pressure of his knees, teaching it little by little the tireless allure which must give it the world and lead it surely to Eden, whose only path there is known to Jehovah alone. Because Israel has preferred many masters to a single master, Jehovah has humiliated it under many yokes, he's rendered it puny, emaciated, ridiculous among nations; in a manner that at present Israel with its sparkling Jerusalem on its hill finds its exact image in this mare, Herodias, in this Jezebel, rawboned, painted, who whinnies at Machaerus, under a diseased rider! But you have exhausted my patience, says Jehovah! You have even exhausted my laughter, Jerusalem; the agony of Israel soothes my heart. I am going to send you a Messiah you weren't expecting, sick man! And the nations will rejoice over the one who will be the terror of Israel. You thought you were called, but it's been a long while, since I, Jehovah, repented! Did you take me for a complaisant spouse accepting the surplus profits of your prostitution? Thief, did you expect to find in me the accomplice of your illicit commerce, taking the tithe of your usury from the blood and sweat of the poor? Did you think to corrupt me with your incense, with your Temple, with your music? Am I a god to be flattered, caressed, slept with? I am the God who made the Leviathan. I hold life in my right hand and death in my left. I have a whip of a hundred straps for the rebellious people. War and famine and all the plagues, I abandon to their will, I set them free. Let it snort its science and its sensuality. I laugh to see it bathe itself in death. Go, do your will, Israel. Go dance some more. I already hear the lugubrious laugh of the hyena living alone in Galilee, reigning in Jerusalem alone, and the howlings of the coyote who feasts in the ruins of the Holy of Holies.

CROWD: Pity! Pity!

JOHN: From North and South, from East and West, it's coming and rushing on; war, purveyors of vultures; in the turned up flap of her dress, she holds murder, arson and devastation. She sows, the good planter, the only grain called by your labors. Here she is, the companion of Christ, she's coming, she's coming, the servant of the Messiah; she's coming one day, the bold woman, into your houses and your hovels, she's coming to do the work of cleansing that you have too long deferred, rich and poor of Israel! And only the dwellings of those marked by sheep's blood will be spared. And here, War, will increase the roaring of widows and mothers, and the hymn of all nations glorifying the Christ by admiring your punishment, as Zion bleeds to death amidst the moving shroud of sand.

THE CROWD: Pity! Pity! Baptism! Ah, God! Ah! God!

JOHN: It's vain for you to clasp your infants to your hearts, O mothers, or to hide them in the arms of your husband, O wives, to raise your arms to heaven, old geezers, to scream pity, young girls. With a violent hand they will be torn from you, those children, those spouses, those lovers, and the burning breath of simoon that is running through the confines of the desert cannot hide from its grasp nor from its burning all this virile flesh which had eyes only for you, hands only for you, heart only to adore you, will only in the service of your swooning, that never puts on its glory except to make you scream with sensuality and to burst into weeping with lovers that have never known a shiver of fear except at the creaking of your sandals and the soft rustle of your skirts. Pity for you, women? Pity for them? Pitiless couple, couple absorbed in yourself, you never had pity for yourself nor for the man engulfed by your pleasure! Seeing you in your distress Adam fell. You would never have come close to your companion except with trembling, and you would have wept, shouted to God to see the terrible nursery of your work. O Israel, carefree people, you have begot children without bothering yourself to assure them the cares and vigilance of a paternity less precarious than yours; and you taught them there is no other God except man, and that there is no other society but that of man, no other security but that of Kings, no other sweetness except in the embrace of a woman. Then perish Israel for neglecting to adore on your knees, face in the dust, the imperishable force.

THE CROWD: (prostrate) Jehovah God, pity!

JOHN: Jehovah God, I seek your face!! How will I see the splendor of your Christ, how will I see him come down from the mountain enveloped by dawn, enshielded with light! Jerusalem of the pure, I admire you, Royal Zion, reverberating with canticles, immutable throne of a God who is the conqueror of death. Blessed Earth, Earth fecund in joy, immortal Canaan, sojourn of an Israel purified by fire, regenerated by spirit, behold my repenting flock, that I drive toward your pastures, and toward your shining waters! O nameless sweetness of living! Very sweet and musical face of a shepherd. Behold the humble ones I bring you! So as to give them incorruptible nourishment, here are the lamenters of Israel that I am bringing you to dry their tears and so you may make kings of them! (he comes down)

THE CROWD: Baptism, O prophet, Baptism.

JOHN: Then descend into the Jordan and we will baptize you by the grace of Jehovah! Simon, Jonathan, Eleazer, immerse all those who present themselves to you. But know indeed, people, that Jehovah God is not a man to disappoint and that he demands, for admitting you to the elect of his Christ, complete repentance. Absolute subjection, without reserve, to his laws. Forget your will.

(Eleazer, Jonathan and Simon and many others leave.)

A PUBLICAN: What must I do to be saved, Master?

JOHN: Who are you?

PUBLICAN: A contemptible man, a publican, a collector of taxes for the Romans.

JOHN: Practice your profession without fraud and may

the money that soils your hands not attach itself to your heart. Keep yourself from being harsh to your brothers so that Jehovah won't be pitiless to you.

A SOLDIER: Master, will I be saved? What must I do?

JOHN: Soldier, earn your wages by serving those who pay you. Do exactly what is commanded but don't lend your arm to the wish for blood. For you, in the baseness of your condition, O mercenary, there are great reasons to hope.

SIMON: Who are you, you who baptize and insult your betters?

JOHN: Pharisee, I am a Jew like you, like you a son of Abraham, but not believing myself, as you do, justified and worthy of being messiah from the simple fact I am a Jew.

NATHANIEL: But who are you? The Messiah? Certainly not, you are too ignorant.

JOHN: The Messiah? I am not worthy of undoing the laces of his boots. But, as for me, my ignorance doesn't give me satisfaction, and I am not speaking of enthroning the son of David, nor do I flatter myself with the hope of being his first minister or his high priest.

JOSEPH: You know that the Messiah must be preceded by Elijah the prophet?

JOHN: I know it.

NICODEMUS: Then, are you Elijah?

JOHN: I am a voice that cries out in the desert.

NICODEMUS: But still?

JOHN: Do you know what you are? Do I know what I am? Perhaps God has designated you to be his interpreter and commentator on his law. He only told me, "Announce what is going to happen and exhort Israel to mend its ways." I wasn't placed here by my own will, but a will is in me which orders me to cry out like the wind shaking the reeds of this Jordan River.

SIMON: He's a fool. Come, we are wasting our time.

NATHANIEL: He's possessed of the devil; his name is frenzy.

(They exit.)

NICODEMUS: For my part; obstinacy or perhaps a fatal hardening of heart.

JOSEPH: I don't know what shame keeps me from asking him for baptism.

JOHN: (to Barzilai and his wife) Ploughman, may your spirit not be completely in your fields. It's not you who impel the ear of corn. You owe your sweat to the earth, but only your sweat; receive from Jehovah God all the rest. Know how to pray; observe the repose of the seventh day; this day will nourish your soul. All the others nourish only the body.

JOSEPH: He's orthodox.

NICODEMUS: His heart is eloquent, too.

BARZILAI: Now, indeed, cousin, are you coming? What are you waiting for?

(Jesus approaches.)

JOHN: And you? Andrew, we will come down. Oh! Oh! This one here. This face. I've seen him. Am I sleeping? Am I myself? You are still here, Pharisees? It's only a vision. He's no longer there. Behold Machaerus, black on the heavens, Is he still there? Is he dead?

ANDREW: Master, won't you speak to this man? He's Jesus, he's a Nazarene like you. He's coming from Galilee.

JOHN: A little later.

ANDREW: He's waiting, master.

JOHN: Have you noticed nothing in him? To compare him to other men or to me?

ANDREW: I don't know.

JOHN: Rabbi, what do you want from me?

JESUS: Baptism.

JOHN: Baptism is for the impure.

JESUS: Baptize me then.

JOHN: You are pure.

JESUS: With this flesh?

JOHN: It's I, it's I who ought to ask baptism of you.

JESUS: Let us each do what is commanded of us. You are hesitating, John. And at first you turned away from me. Obeying, I came. Can you refuse yourself to a son of man? The furor of God has stirred you up, lion, against the rebel will. Is there still in you some fragment of will?

JOHN: Is it for me to baptize the son of David?

JESUS: And since it pleases the Father that you baptize the son of David?

JOHN: I will baptize you then, but I've recognized you.

JESUS: Happy are you, John, that God makes you so

clearly confident.

JOHN: Mine eyes have seen the day! O Israel, I sense dancing on the earth! The day! The Day! And no more night! Andrew, and you others, Pharisees, the King.

JESUS: Shut up, John. Let Jehovah God choose his hour. Eyes won't be opened by your joy. Don't scandalize the creature.

JOHN: Andrew! Andrew! This is the one that must be followed.

JESUS: Are you forgetting those you called to baptism? And who are awaiting you with tears?

JOHN: Desert—here is glory! (Exit Jesus) O you, all the dead, quicken with cheer. All sepulchers sing! Let all be life and joy and psalms! Enslaved Israel, even your ashes, may they exult, and let there be only one Israel, triumphant, with millions of mouths singing and millions of lyres.

(Exit John and Andrew.)

NICODEMUS: I am confounded. All that I've seen and heard today, this crowd, this voice which makes you shiver, and this taciturn man.

JOSEPH: I need to reflect on all this. We will talk about it, friend, with a rested mind at your place or mine. One mustn't accept or reject everything rashly.

NICODEMUS: I shall return. I begin to think there is more wisdom in the desert than in the synagogue.

JOSEPH: Prudence, friend, prudence.

(They leave. Kanthera and soldiers enter.)

KANTHERA: This is it. Nobody. Explore this cave. (two soldiers enter the grotto) Who's watching the horses?

A SOLDIER: Iacim.

KANTHERA: The Tetrarch forbids mistreating him.

SECOND SOLDIER: They are all there splashing around in the river.

(Soldiers come out of the grotto.)

THIRD SOLDIER: No one. Mathan found a book on a bed of dry leaves.

FOURTH SOLDIER: Here it is.

KANTHERA: Give it here. "I will sow your bones around your altars. The day of Jehovah is approaching. There will be only a single pastor, my servant, David; they will know I am Jehovah.—" Stupidity of these Israelites! Fanatic nation! that used to live in Babylon.

What good was Jehovah when you were living in Babylon? (tossing the book away) The dog always returns to its vomit. As for me, I'm Jehovah. Yuck! Baal's worth more and Astarte; there's some humanity in these gods.

SECOND SOLDIER: The beast is coming.

KANTHERA: Alone?

SECOND SOLDIER: With two others.

KANTHERA: Hide. You've got the rope?

THIRD SOLDIER: Here it is.

KANTHERA: No blows or wounds. I will whistle. Be prompt. Go. (the soldiers leave) Nebuchadnezzar was similarly housed during seven years of his madness. Beast to sorrow, man. I don't know what philosopher said that. He has the appearance of being beside himself. Is this one here a saint or a monkey? (he hides)

JOHN: And what do I care what Barzilai says? They are always the son of somebody. The tree is judged by its fruit. And didn't Saul find a crown, tending the asses of his father? And wasn't David a shepherd?

ELEAZER: We know your work; and this Jesus didn't open his mouth. He only made an appearance and behold, Andrew, your favorite, and his simple brother Simon, left you to follow him.

JOHN: Many others yet will leave me. As he grows, so must I diminish. And when I shall be all alone here, and all Israel shall have forgotten the way to my cavern, as for me, I will disappear, to speak, to sing, to dance, like David before the ark, without fear that the savage beasts and the gazelles be scandalized, as Michael once did.

JONATHAN: You won't leave us?

JOHN: I won't drive you out. But soon there will echo the resounding, strident, the cry of the trumpet. And you will have wings to run to Jerusalem. Prepare your ears to hear it. For in those times the desert will return to its legitimate inhabitants, the wild beasts, while Israel is eating with its king in his dwelling and under his lighted pavilions.

KANTHERA: Lovely trio of idiots! (he whistles) Is it you they call John?

JOHN: It's me.

KANTHERA: Bind him! (the soldiers tie John) Excuse my impertinence, prophet! Tetrarch's orders! Herod Antipas demands the privilege of hearing you and wants to be alone to rejoice in your conversation. The cage is prepared; no need to yell and scream. None are deaf at Machaerus, and Antipas is benevolent. Thus the chagrin of knowing that another Daniel is celebrated in his provinces and not sleeping every night on feathers. Is it done? Make way, you others! March!

JOHN: For him to increase, I must diminish.

KANTHERA: That's well said. You are resigned—about time.

JOHN: Antipas is really imprudent.

KANTHERA: It's not bathers in the Jordan who will take Machaerus. Antipas defies a siege.

JOHN: (carried away) One doesn't defy God, man, one doesn't defy God!

(They leave.)

ELEAZER: This is done by Israel!

JONATHAN: Let us follow, brothers, let us follow.

CURTAIN

ACT I

SCENE 2: THE PRISON IN THE FORTRESS OF MACHAERUS

A cell.

(John is asleep, enchained. The Jailor enters.)

JAILOR: The master is coming. Get up, animal! On your feet!

(Enter Antipas.)

ANTIPAS: What a stench! Where is he?

JAILOR: Here before you, master.

ANTIPAS: Go open the air hole.

JAILOR: You intend to remain alone with him, master?

ANTIPAS: Isn't he chained? Go. (Jailor exits) John, listen

to me. Are you sleeping?

JOHN: I am listening.

ANTIPAS: Can't you hold yourself up? I came to talk to you. My Roman guests are sleeping. I am only thinking of you, without hate, tormented by knowing that the message you have for me, and that you are going to communicate to me in a reasonable language and no longer in the barbarous style in which you flagellate your half-witted auditors by the Jordan. I am listening to you and here are my questions. Who are you? Who is this Messiah that you are announcing? What does your baptism signify? And why did you say to my wife, "The days of Herod Antipas are over."? Answer me without rage in the way I am questioning you. If you are a prophet, say so, and I will honor you as such. Prove to me that you come from Jehovah and in an hour you will be free. Free to insult me, more free than I am. Well? Are you dead? There are no chains except on your members. Your tongue isn't. Man, I do not have a lot of time. Vitellius is going to have me called. Speak as you wish or as you can. What's become of your audacity? Has inspiration deserted you? This man, overcome by his chains, is he the man who put Herodias in a fury and made the Synagogue tremble? On such a fine occasion to speak, and then scorn it. Jehovah has abandoned you? Or rather how must one interpret your silence? Is your silence also prophetic? Is it the scorn of an ascetic for the man enslaved by the flesh? But if you are from God, as I am tempted to believe, you cannot scorn a sinner even if he is Tetrarch. All sinners have a right to the pity of the just; for the most just of mortals is not just enough to set himself up in judgment, and you are mortal and a man. The odor of your cells proves that. And if your silence is from condemnation, it is I who will condemn you on the last day. You don't wish to speak? You think me uncurable? You are thinking, Herod is the prisoner of his vice. God has hardened the heart of this new Pharaoh, the Egyptian plagues won't lead him to repentance. He's a dead man and one cannot revive the dead. But if you are a prophet recall the widow of Sarepta and the prophet who revived her dead child. Is it something impossible to God? And aren't you conceiving some hope from the fact I voluntarily came down to this shadow? That's fine. Your guardian will inform me if some day you desire to speak to me. You are the master of your fate. Prophet, you are free. I will protect you and no one will attempt your life in the province of my power. Impostor or madman, it's indeed necessary that you expiate the boldness of your tongue. (starts to leave and returns) You are not a prophet. It's written. "The prophet is recognized by the fulfillment of the prophecy." It reminds me, that is written. You said, "The Messiah is come!" Where is he? Indeed, you know that he hasn't come, and it's your lie that grasps your throat. If the Son of David had appeared, Machaerus is not so far from Jerusalem that I wouldn't have heard the voice of his precursor. And what have I heard from my walls? Only the drumming of caravans and the reverberant echo of your howling! Your silence—where was my head in trying to explain it otherwise? Your confusion causes me pity. Israel has not yet any other king than Caesar; the seat of the precursor is still vacant at each Israelite table, and the Temple is still waiting for the Son of David!

JOHN: (standing) I have seen him.

ANTIPAS: Don't shout! Is it with this furious tone the truth is spoken?

JOHN: The one who is struck by lightning, doesn't see the flash. Jehovah is blinding you and deafening you to strike you the more surely. You see nothing, you hear nothing, because your eye and your ear, all enchanted by sensuality, obstructed by luxury, and the flesh, at the vapid and cruel odor, weaves around you a thick vapor, heavy like the night. There is no spirit to hear spirit or to see spirit. For example, do you see me? No, you see a hairy beast who bears himself in a grotesque or terrible manner. Are you hearing me? No—you are hearing only words without consequences, a thunder of discordant noise. How then will you see the Christ and how will you understand him? At the very time his light pierces the opaque cloud you will be stinking in the mist in which you are rolling like a drunkard in the mud. Before you have a chance to ask, "What's this light?", you will be dying, you will cease to be, absolutely, if one can name being this seething agitation of shapelessness, this total absence of spirit. You will be on the ground, mouth still full of meat, asking yourself, "What's happening to me?" See the Christ! You won't even see a man, when, looking at me, you see only a beast, or looking at yourself in the steel of a mirror you admire a Tetrarch. But if the blindfold falls from your eyes and I could surgically remove from you this unheard of cataract, seeing there all of us, the man, the beast, and the Tetrarch, you would recognize at your cost, the King, the Precursor, and you must seek a name which doesn't exist to name what I see, and the sight which made me ill.

ANTIPAS: You have spoken at length and you haven't responded to one of my questions.

JOHN: Didn't I tell you that you are deaf? I announced the Christ; the Christ has appeared, yes, the son of David, the King, the Messiah and you are condemned to death if you don't repent and don't stop the adultery.

ANTIPAS: Prove that the Christ has appeared.

JOHN: I saw him, I tell you.

ANTIPAS: But no one else but you?

JOHN: Many others beside.

ANTIPAS: Who? The Doctors? The Pharisees? Machaerus is full of them; they haven't announced the event to me.

JOHN: It isn't from blindness that the blind will—

ANTIPAS: Come on! Come on! The Messiah must be recognized by all.

JOHN: My disciples have recognized him. They had only to see him and they followed him.

ANTIPAS: But at least the works of the Messiah must publish his arrival. The Tetrarchy is calm; no emotion in Judea is discernible.

JOHN: Authorize those who wish to see me to enter your fort and even my cell. Before entering I charged two of my disciples to observe and report the deeds of Christ and his actions. You will be able to hear them enumerated; acts that will make Caesar blanch!

ANTIPAS: You haven't been prisoner for a day. No one yet has presented himself to see you. And I repeat to you that Judea is calm, so also is Galilee. The ploughman at his harvest, the drover with his flock, the artisan in his shop, the doctor in his Synagogue, the Priest in the Temple. Not a soul that exists from Damas to Hebron suspects the existence of the prophesized King. I want to believe in your sincerity. But truly, you are prey to an illusion. What's his name? The one you think you saw.

JOHN: Does one ask the name of Jehovah's Christ?

ANTIPAS: But where's he come from?

JOHN: From Galilee.

ANTIPAS: But the Messiah must come from Judah. Are you unaware of the scriptures?

JOHN: I didn't ask him the place of his birth.

ANTIPAS: But then?

JOHN: I saw his face and I trembled. And I recognized the Son of David.

ANTIPAS: And what did he say?

JOHN: Nothing.

ANTIPAS: And what was he going to do at the Jordan? Is it you he was seeking?

JOHN: Me, and the baptism of repentance.

ANTIPAS: Baptism? The Messiah asked you for baptism? And you, you baptized the Messiah?

JOHN: I baptized him.

ANTIPAS: Mockery.

JOHN: I am not one of those who dispute the command of God.

ANTIPAS: And you believe?

JOHN: Yes, I believe, I believe! Get behind me, Satan! Go ask your sluts, oracles who you cannot doubt. Question your Pharisees. In a thousand years they will tell you that the Messiah is yet to come? They only believe in a Messiah who is a scholar like themselves, ignorant like themselves, quarrelsome like themselves, and who will allow himself to be taken in by their humbug piety. One who will shut his eyes to their domestic debauches and who will crown their pride. And you can only believe in a Christ who's friends with Caesar and who will allow you to remain in Machaerus and be merry at your pleasure.

ANTIPAS: And you—?

JOHN: I believe in a Christ who demands a rigorous account from me; who incarnates the Law, who rewards and punishes according to justice, who sees the heart and tests the depths, and who contains in himself and transfigures in himself the virtue of Abraham, of Joseph, of Samuel, and of David and all of ancient Israel.

ANTIPAS: And that one won't demand baptism of you, and he won't come from Galilee, and he won't allow you to rot in the bottom of a pit?

JOHN: He will do his will. But I have faith in his justice; he won't forget me in this darkness, and he won't let me die without having seen his glory.

ANTIPAS: What must I do to see him, me too, and be spared?

JOHN: Return me to the desert, to your brother, his wife, and comprehend the enormity of your crime and the scandal.

ANTIPAS: Too many crimes flourish in Israel for it to be scandalized by mine. Phillip? He lives in Rome and he cares for his wife the way I do for his mistresses or freedmen. Why should I return to him what he doesn't ask for or want? And you speak easily of freeing you, who never possessed anything and might envy a poor man his dog. Flesh, love, sensuality, what are these to you except words, words and cadavers of flowers! You don't know what the sweetness of the bosom or the heat of a shared bed is, of embracing, in swooning between two fragile and beautiful female flanks. You've never done anything but look in the stars, slept on a stone, known other kisses than the sting of a mosquito. Have you ever laughed? You are only a primitive man, so simplified that you cannot understand the needs, the thoughts, the sorrows of men. You shrug your shoulders? Companion of tigresses, you advise me very easily to send away the woman who crossed the sea and desert to rejoin me, and who brings me all that the savage, the taciturn daughter of Arabia can never give me.

JOHN: Lucky still to have only such a feeble duty. To have only to cut yourself away from a vice!

ANTIPAS: But my vice belongs to me! Can I repent of being who I am and coming from a luxurious blood? Rather repent being born. Are we responsible for paternal sins? Go, you know nothing of man and you are only a wild beast. You are creating the Messiah in your own image. But as for me, I say to you the Messiah will be a man or he won't speak unintelligible language, eat grasshoppers, become crazy because of his solitude. If you had known ambition or drunk wine, or caressed the least prostitute, you would know how to speak to human weakness.

JOHN: Antipas, you make me feel pity. Your chains are heavier than mine. Come, return me to the desert, so I don't die and the people won't cry out against you.

ANTIPAS: She doesn't wish it.

JOHN: Tell her I will no longer open my mouth against her or against you.

ANTIPAS: She wants you dead.

JOHN: What's it to her if I live or die?

ANTIPAS: But you will continue to announce the King?

JOHN: It's necessary! It's necessary. What's holding you back? Release me! Do you know what you are doing by opposing Jehovah? Let me go or my word will bring ruin on you and all Machaerus. Do you think whatever may be the art of your mason it prevents these stones from being disjoined? I say to you it is God. Let him extend his arm and your dwelling is only a ruin. Your Herodias wants me to die? The same Jehovah who laughed seeing Machaerus grow, this heap of stones, made my body and he made the knot which links my body and my soul, and to disjoin them it takes another will than that of your wench and another axe than that of your executioner. I tell you this. I cannot die before having seen the glory of Christ and the fulfillment of his word that I have prophesized. Let me then go, from fear that Jehovah, to loosen my chain, may not be constrained to loosen all Machaerus! And do you think you can prevent him?

ANTIPAS: You've seen the son of David?

JOHN: I've seen him! I've seen him!

ANTIPAS: You won't call out outside?

JOHN: It's necessary I see his glory and that I purify his people.

ANTIPAS: I will authorize your messengers to bring you news. And your disciples will end by purifying the people.

JOHN: Begone! I am weary of speaking to a sepulcher. (lies down)

ANTIPAS: In a sepulcher, you mean. (Jailor enters) What is it?

JAILOR: Master, a man has just been arrested, who succeeded, no one knows how, in sneaking into the fortress; questioned, he said his name is Jonathan and only came to see the prisoner.

JOHN: Antipas, make him come! Ah, ah! Curious to hear news of Christ, bring this Jonathan down if you dare! He's one of those I sent.

ANTIPAS: Bring this man. (the Jailor exits)

JOHN: Herod Antipas, here is my deliverance and your death. If you have ears, hear! And if you are afraid, you must indeed have dungeons deeper than these? The time has come for you to descend into it. Ask the entrails of rock to open. I fear now that Jehovah won't remove you from your nest yet. He has a sharp eye and an astute ear. He knows better than I how to shock your heart against your sides, and he sees the worm attack the heap of your vertebrae. With senses less acute, I only hear the chattering of your teeth as they clash. Repent, man, repent, simplify yourself. Here's news of the one who simplifies in the extreme, the most complicated life, the best dressed, the best disguised. (enter Jonathan with the Jailor) Speak, Jonathan, speak. And don't be upset by the presence of this Tetrarch. Don't make him languish.

JONATHAN: Rabbi, I haven't been able to join the man

of Galilee. And, after having discussed with Simon and Andrew who followed him I no longer care to approach him; I was anxious about your fate, more than seeing or hearing about this Jesus!

ANTIPAS: Ah!

JOHN: What do you know about him?

JONATHAN: He said that the kingdom is not of this world and that no one, if not reborn from water and from spirit can enter the kingdom, and he boasted if the Temple were to be destroyed to rebuild it in three days.

ANTIPAS: John is no longer listening to you. Answer me if you wish to live. Who is this man?

JONATHAN: His name's Jesus; he's the son of a carpenter from Nazareth in Galilee.

ANTIPAS: Fine. You don't think he can be the Messiah?

JONATHAN: The Messiah! Certainly not! Would the Messiah speak of a kingdom not of this world? It's fine for Simon and Andrew to think that a Galilean like themselves could be the Messiah.

ANTIPAS: But as for you? Who do you think he is? A prophet?

JONATHAN: There's only one prophet: John. I beg you

to set him free.

ANTIPAS: We shall see. Come with me. You will eat your fill. You have pleased me, and I will give the order to let you communicate with your master if you wish. Come. Goodbye, John. You make me pity, man.

(Jonathan, Antipas and the Jailor leave.)

JOHN: (prostrated) A, a, ah! Ao, ah! Jehovah, why have you abandoned me? O divine treason and more than human mockery! It's really you, I recognized you! Pouncing on me like a vulture you've torn my flesh, you've planted me in the sand and commanded me to bellow his coming! He's coming! You haven't released me. You've dried my eyes and desiccated my heart, and you filled me with great power to shout ceaselessly, like a beast with burning entrails. You've driven me from life, you've given me the desert to live in and you've said to me, "Parade about like a cloud between heaven and earth to shock men by your horrible appearance and your thunderous spittings, ruminate without end the bitter grass of my word! And when Israel will come and you have indeed despaired of it, you will depict to it the source of the oasis and the face of the Messiah and they will be deceived like a caravan by a mirage; and I will laugh with you and at them, as I laughed having driven Adam from the garden, saying, 'Behold, Adam has become one of us through knowledge of good and evil.?'" And you placed at the Garden of Eden the Cherubims and the flaming sword whirling so that the man, dressed by you in the garb of animals, would never approach the Tree of Life. O misery of created man, immense, incurable, eternal! And this Jesus, naive like me, full like me of a great dream; to what cell, to what gibbet, to what bitter disillusionment have you reserved for him, this child who only wanted to do your will? O lamentable Israel, it was useless to tell you in a sweeter and more fraternal voice. O millions of my brothers in distress, blind suffering multitude that I didn't love enough and to whom I was announcing a tyrant worse than Herod! What are we, O my people, ploughers of arid soil, workers from birth, only a lost flock under the storm cloud trumpeting Messiah! In the dark of an eternal shadow! O message of a reign of glory, phantom child of solitary ardor and the laughter of God! Carnal dream of a stunning Christ, of a new David and of a terrestrial Jerusalem that I wanted to prefigure, and I intended to suggest the attitude of your immutable will toward it, Jehovah! But your light is our shadow and your Christ will not establish his domination according to the fashion of our imaginations. Wouldn't it have been better for me to have divined this; this Galilean saying, "The Kingdom is not of this world."? Pride of man that boasts of having no pride. It's necessary that I diminish! As if I were higher than my brothers. And by what right then do I have this arrogant, chiding tone? Equal in ignorance, O our misery! To love, to love! Is that what you want, obscure Master Jehovah? Yes, that's it. And you've pulled me out of it, put me in the dock because I didn't give you satisfaction! Give me life, Eternal one, give me life, even for a short while! Bad luck to whoever doesn't love! Bad luck to the hard heart that doesn't open to the thundering voice of love! O God! You compel it at the point of the sword, you shut it in prickly haircloth, on all sides, bloodying it.

(Jonathan returns.)

JONATHAN: Master! Master!

JOHN: Free, Jonathan? You are weeping? Herod? I summon you to speak. Is it the tears of wine already? What have you to tell me that's so funereal?

JONATHAN: Herodias' daughter danced—

JOHN: Salome? I know she dances. Otherwise than the women of your village, otherwise than the angels.

JONATHAN: May the Eternal curse her!

JOHN: Shut up! The Eternal is not at your orders. Perhaps she danced for my well being.

JONATHAN: For your ruin.

JOHN: Speak then. Are you a prophet, too?

JONATHAN: Antipas shouted, "Ask half my kingdom, I swear to grant it to you."

JOHN: Jehovah, I recognize your hand.

JONATHAN: The daughter ran to her mother and she came back saying, "O Master"—.

JOHN: O God!

JONATHAN: "I want you to give me the head of John the Baptist."

JOHN: Ah!

JONATHAN: Shocked, I came in horror to hear Herod's reply. Oh! Salome! I will see her dance until my death; I will die of having seen her. She is beautiful! And all the looks that possessed her under her veils. Oh, Master! The patience of Jehovah! They are coming. She! He consented.

JOHN: Salome? Salome, here?

(Enter Salome with a basin, the Jailor and the Executioner with a naked blade.)

JAILOR: Don't come in, Mistress. This is not a sight for your eyes.

SALOME: I want to see him.

JOHN: It's God who sends you, Salome, to hear me. Obedient to the maternal order you asked for my head, obedient to the order of Jehovah, Salome, you will demand my life. You are Jewish, right? Jewish like Esther,

Jewish like Judith and your God, like the God of Esther and Judith is Jehovah. Daughter of Israel, it's up to you to save Israel one more time. O Salome, your dance, it is our God who taught it to you to save his prophet. Israel dies if I die. I who know the words of life. You will dance once more before Herod, and for reward you will demand the salvation of Israel, that I, and I alone, can save. What happiness would you gain from my death, right? And Jehovah himself, recalling your dance, if you don't turn it to the salvation of his prophet. You know that I must announce the Messiah and prepare all the people for his reign. Otherwise, Israel will be entirely lost, overthrown—and with Israel, you, Salome, your mother, and Antipas—if the last prophet were to die without having spoken. Life is nothing to me, Salome. If the Messiah had appeared, I would give myself up to the knife without a word. But Jehovah's getting impatient with my silence, and it is he who presses me to do his work. In his name, I adjure you, Salome, more beautiful than Esther, stronger than Judith,—by dancing, nothing but dancing, and not by the lengthy prostitution of Esther, nor by handling of the sword for which your childish hands would be too delicate, by dancing before a new Asahareus, what glory will fall to you, Serving Girl of the Eternal, and with what honor you are going to surround the Messiah-King, the one who is coming, the Son of David! Go back, Salome, dance once more, and revoke the order of death that God will avenge on your posterity—if his rage wills you to have posterity!

SALOME: I am much too weary to dance. I don't know

Jehovah, nor Esther, nor Judith.

JAILOR: Strike, Manassah. The Master's going to get impatient.

JOHN: Stand back! Salome, go tell Antipas that he has nothing to fear from me. Let him live! Let him jubilate! What does his lechery matter to me! May my tongue dry up if I speak against him again! It has other words to say! Don't approach, brute, or I will crush you with my chains. Take a step, I command hell to open beneath his feet! Salome, go back or I will curse you! Obtain my life! Go, prostitute yourself, practice Sodom and Gomorrah, but don't soil yourself with human blood! Jehovah! Jehovah! Make known your will. Well, go on, brute! Go on little girl—

VOICE: (From outside) Get back! Let me pass!

JOHN: Eleazer!

(Enter Eleazer.)

ELEAZER: Master, I've seen the Messiah! I've spoken to him.

JOHN: Jesus of Nazareth?

ELEAZER: That's him! On your behalf, I asked him, "Are you the one who must come or must we wait for another?" And at that moment he had cured the ill and the possessed. And he said to me, "Tell John what you have seen and heard: the blind can see, the crippled are walking, the lepers are purified, the deaf can hear, the dead revive, the poor are evangelized." Oh, John and then he said—

JOHN: (to the Executioner) Hold on a minute, brother. Sister, tell him to be patient for a moment.

ELEAZER: "The one who believes in the Son has eternal life and the one who doesn't, won't have life, and those baptized by John have justified God, for whom John is a prophet, the greatest of the sons of woman."

JOHN: It's him! It's him! I saw him. For him to be believed it's necessary for me to be diminished, for me to disappear. The hope of the earth is accomplished! The scream of my bowels is exhausted.

ELEAZER: And he said, "He who loses his life on account of me will be saved."

JOHN: Then no tears! Brother, take my head. Let the child take it to her stupid mother on the plate.

SALOME: He's laughing and those there are weeping.

(The Executioner brandishes his sword.)

ELEAZER AND JONATHAN: Jehovah!

CURTAIN

ACT II

SCENE 3: THE RESURRECTION OF LAZARUS

Bethany, in front of the house of Lazarus.

Judas enters. Magdalene comes from the house.

MAGDALENE: You, Judas? Alone?

JUDAS: Your brother?

MAGDALENE: Dead.

JUDAS: What?

MAGDALENE: Lazarus is dead.

JUDAS: When?

MAGDALENE: Day before yesterday, in the morning.

JUDAS: This is a prophecy.

MAGDALENE: Is the Master coming?

JUDAS: He will see the invisible.

MAGDALENE: Judas!

JUDAS: He cannot prevent it. He can do nothing to prevent it.

MAGDALENE: The death of Lazarus affects you to this degree, Judas?

JUDAS: Surely. Where is Martha?

MAGDALENE: By the sepulcher, weeping.

JUDAS: And you are staying at the house?

MAGDALENE: Some one has to. The Master will come, Judas.

JUDAS: He's coming with Simon, John and Andrew.

MAGDALENE: When will he be here?

JUDAS: Before evening. So many folks on the way are stopping him. But will you be able to receive the five of us tonight? I don't understand why he made me ask you that. Hospitality is not required of two women in mourning.

MAGDALENE: He is always welcome. Even if we may not sleep tonight, my sister and I, you five will all repose.

JUDAS: Great love!

MAGDALENE: It would be nice to see the Messiah rejected at our door, consolation disdained.

JUDAS: Words!

MAGDALENE: The only ones that are not vain, his words. The only ones which tears obey.

JUDAS: Listen to me.

MAGDALENE: I am going to inform Martha.

JUDAS: Can't you hear other words than his?

MAGDALENE: You, who follow him; do you hear other words than his?

JUDAS: He no longer says anything but obscure things that scandalize, that make one suspect he may be the One who we believed—

MAGDALENE: The Messiah.

JUDAS: The Messiah-King, the Foretold-One; if he is, why does he speak so often of death? Is this a mortal king we are expecting? Mortal and poor? I have no more than three deniers in the common purse. After three years, the Pharisees and the great have not recognized him. Only the very low, the weak—

MAGDALENE: You love him less, Judas—

JUDAS: It's well enough for you to love. As for me, I think.

MAGDALENE: O Judas, don't go back. You renounced everything to follow him and from that day, by possessing nothing, you possessed everything. If I were living like you, his friend, in his shadow, if I constantly heard his word, the only one that seems living and certain among dead and dangerous words, I would be happy, peaceful, like a little child, without many memories, without desires, without thought. The rest of you men love badly; you never forget yourselves. As for him, Judas, he always forgets himself.

JUDAS: A man ought never to abandon himself. What a dupe! You and I, we are not made of the same material. Before being a servant girl in your brother's home, for money, you were a servant girl for every man. If the Nazarene had begged you for love you would not have refused, so today, indeed, you content yourself with pretty words.

MAGDALENE: He knows us too well to beg us for love. Rather to love a flower or the innocent animal. My heart would laugh to see men trembling before my face.

JUDAS: You are weeping?

MAGDALENE: As for him, when he looked at me, I saw myself quite wretched, completely sinful, eaten by worms. And seeing me, such as I was, he did not turn away in disgust. He neither cursed me nor condemned me.

JUDAS: By what right? He's neither priest nor doctor. You are imagining things.

MAGDALENE: You no longer believe, Judas.

JUDAS: I believed; my misery believed. He enrolled us with promises. He must establish the kingdom. He appeared to be someone mysterious; nothing ought to be impossible to him. They expected much of a man who only had to look at you to know your thoughts. He sees, perhaps, he knows everything; but he can prevent nothing. He saw the death of Lazarus; three days ago as we were walking in the country, he stopped and said, "Lazarus is dead."

MAGDALENE: It was three days ago.

JUDAS: He sees his own death; he doesn't prevent that either. He is unable to prevent anything. All he has is words. The poor folk are satisfied with them. The others laugh and shrug their shoulders. He can do nothing, nor can he undo anything. He's only a beggar who speaks, who cannot prevent the world from going its way. Whoever has a hope, a wish, intelligence, let him avoid meeting this persuasive beggar, this seducer without hearth or home; he will conceive a hope out of proportion to his small hope, a desire that will turn him away from his small desire and from thoughts capable of bursting his small intelligence. He will deliver himself to his care to conduct him, and he'll permit himself to be led down roads without end, into the unknown, into the void. Further, always further from all desire, from all hope, from all that the hand can touch, from all that reason can conceive, far from the smiles of women, far from the society of friends and family, far from the warmth of the group—towards the misty image of vain kingdoms, towards nothingness. I don't want that; I say no. I'm stopping myself. I am not the mule nourished on food for thought. Dreams are for the night; I am awake. I will seek the way to reconcile myself with the living, interesting myself in their affairs and interesting them in mine.

MAGDALENE: Why continue to follow him? That's not honest, Judas.

JUDAS: That's my affair.

MAGDALENE: O sad heart! To be with him, isn't that the kingdom? (enter Jesus, John, Andrew and Peter) Rabbi, your serving woman.

JESUS: Rise up, woman.

MAGDALENE: Lord, if you had come in time, my brother would not be dead.

PETER: Then it's true? Lazarus is dead?

MAGDALENE: For three days already, regretting not being able to hold your hand in his.

ANDREW: He's weeping.

PETER: How he loved him.

MAGDALENE: Will you come again, Master, now that we are here alone, two poor women who had only him? We had no relatives and I don't know what's going to become of us. As for me, I will go to work at the homes of foreigners; but my poor Martha, Master. Don't abandon that child.

JESUS: Where is she?

MAGDALENE: By the sepulcher. Some friends of Lazarus came and are keeping her company. Ah! Master! There are not many brothers who love their sisters the way Lazarus loved us! But you were much more dear to him than us, Lord.

JESUS: And God, much dearer still, Mary; if I didn't owe myself to all our people, if there were no more sick people in Israel, no more despairing, no more blind, I would say to you, "Here, I'm stopping." Would you treat me like a brother? I will work for you. That is forbidden to me! I wasn't born for the happiness of one or two. You and Martha, Mary, you've heard the word of life! It's necessary that all hear it. It's necessary that all be revived; that the prophets be justified; that all the distress of this people may see coming to it He who will separate it from its bitterness and tear it from death's claw. Mary, your tears are not the sour tears of the blind, and you know in what fountain to wash your eyes. How many as yet know only how to howl like a beast when its young are taken from it? You have a father and you know how to speak to him. I belong to all the orphans. Magdalene will you lead me to the tomb where Lazarus is sleeping?

MAGDALENE: Where he's sleeping, Lord?

JESUS: Yes, where he's sleeping. You are looking at me, John, son of thunder! Don't you know yet that for God, death does not exist? Judas, don't be scandalized by what I am saying: the most ancient dead of Israel, in the most long forgotten sepulchers haven't known death if they've known God. Those living, who breath and plot evil are more dead than the ashes of Jacob. Mary, your brother is sleeping, and they were in too much of a hurry to put him aside. Lead me to the place of his slumber.

MAGDALENE: Master, I am your serving girl! And since you say so, I believe that Lazarus is sleeping.

(All leave except Judas.)

JUDAS: What's he mean and what's he intend to do? If he's going to— Lunatic! It's not a slumber, even a sleep of three days. He must feel. He is indeed dead and I am Judas. He cannot revive Lazarus any more than he can make me a believer like the sons of Jonas and Zebediah, or like this woman with her mad eyes. "Those living who breath and meditate evil—" he's a clairvoyant "are more dead than the ashes of Jacob." But he cannot prevent anything. Let him free himself from the hands in which I am going to put him. That will be the sign. What's he going to do at this tomb? It's well that I learn what he meant.

(Exit)

CURTAIN/BLACKOUT

ACT II

SCENE 4: THE SANHEDRIN

Jerusalem: the Sanhedrin of the Pharisees.

CAIAPHAS: (to Selomith) You've quite understood me? If you find him alone or very few about, you will corner him with your men, and having commanded him to follow you, you will lead him here by a roundabout way. If not, you will wait until the people are dispersed. It's necessary to act without commotion or scandal. I count on your intelligence to seize the opportunity. Go. (exit Selomith) Indeed, we are all agreed, aren't we? We will deliver him to Pilate and we will demand the execution of Jesus.

NICODEMUS: We are putting too much passion into this affair. After an appearance of justice, we are going to demand the death of a man we cannot reproach with anything precise.

DANIEL: Are you, you too, of his disciples?

NICODEMUS: No, Daniel, but I am trying to be fair, and I ask myself if it is just to condemn this Galilean that the people call a great prophet.

SARAI: No prophet ever came out of Galilee.

JOSEPH: You are forgetting Jonas.

PHAROS: Joseph, you are committing an error.

SEMEIAS: All the prophets were Jews.

SARAI: This Galilean a prophet? This ignoramus? This son of a worker?

DANIEL: Was a prophet ever seen to address himself to the little folk?

PHAROS: To banquet with publicans and lost women?

ANOTHER: His disciples are unlettered; they don't know how to read and write.

SARAI: Fishermen.

CAIAPHAS: Listen to us, Nicodemus. I am curious to know how you will defend a man who openly violates the Sabbath, choosing that day of all days to accomplish his pseudo-cures, who pardons adultery, who arrogates to himself to remit sins, who reduces the law to nothingness. What prophet ever did that? By authorizing all that is forbidden by the Law; and haven't I been repeatedly told that he allows himself to be called the son of David and Messiah by the troupe of fanatic imbeciles that he drags about everywhere with him?

ANNAS: The Messiah won't give the lie to Moses; he will crown the law, justify the faith of Abraham and the predictions of the prophets; he won't abrogate the Law. This Galilean speaks against us, against the Temple; he's trying to shake up sacerdotal authority. Are these the characteristics of the Messiah, Nicodemus?

NICODEMUS: Let's question him; let's not condemn him without hearing him.

SEMEIAS: Nicodemus—what have you done with your science?

SARAI: Nicodemus, what have you done with your reason, man?

JOSEPH: Are we losing our reason to want to give fair play?

DANIEL: And you also, Joseph of Arimathea, you believe this Galilean is a prophet?

ANNAS: Brothers, where have your wits gone? Surely, we intend to satisfy the Law. There will be an interrogation, and an appearance of judgment and hearing of witnesses. But how dare you for a single instant take this dreamer from Galilee seriously? I would blush deeply if the shadow of a suspicion flowered in me that this Jesus could be the representative of Jehovah; that this ignorant man was the enunciator of His Will; and I would be overcome with shame on myself if I had for the millionth part of a second believed that this charlatan was the Messiah-King, the Son of David, the Expected One of Israel.

CAIAPHAS: If one of us, Pharisee, priest, or doctor, one day found in the midst of his meditations on the Scriptures, a doubtful prophetic spirit, that would be would be in ever so small a degree, comprehensible; or if I imagined myself, Me, Caiaphas, high priest, maddened by my genealogy to be the Expected One of Israel, madness, but excusable madness. We are close enough to God's thought to experience such vertigoes; but for an unknown, emerging from the depth, head swaddled with shadows to have the pretension of making himself adored not only by the rabble, but by us,—Nicodemus, and you, Joseph, could you seriously think that his case deserved examination? I have trouble understanding your attitude. If we, the brain of Israel, set ourselves to stray, nothing surprising if the people rave wildly with this unanimity in dementia!

NICODEMUS: Our knowledge is then so certain?

SARAI: Intolerable!

ANNAS: Is Nicodemus on the point of promulgating

some new heresy?

NICODEMUS: If he doesn't come from God, by what means does he accomplish such prodigies?

ALL: Through Satan! Enough! He's mad! Silence!

SEMEIAS: What prodigies?

JOSEPH: The blind man he cured?

ALL: Charlatanism! Imposture! He was no more blind than I am! He was possessed by the devil.

CAIAPHAS: In short, where do you propose to go?

NICODEMUS: I want him to be examined.

CAIAPHAS: He will be examined. Is that all?

NICODEMUS: And that, in any case, there will be no question of condemning him to death.

CAIAPHAS: I am stopping you! Nicodemus, don't persist. You will incur excommunication.

ANNAS: This is from madness! Can't you see that if we allow such impostors to roam free, provoking sedition, we are exposing ourselves to the wrath of Rome? Aren't you instructed by events. To spare an agitator do you want to destroy us all?

JOSEPH: But if he is innocent?

ALL: Enough! Exclusion.

CAIAPHAS: Guilty or innocent, it's better for one man to perish than the whole people! And when that man is only a magician of little ability—

SEMEIAS: The fact is they tell strange stories—

(Enter Joel.)

SARAI: I have heard tell that he cures the possessed solely through the imposition of his hands and a fixed look in their eyes.

PHAROS: They told me that a paralytic was able to run and walk without help from others on his order.

NICODEMUS: He has a great ascendancy over crowds. Inexplicable, but that cannot be denied.

CAIAPHAS: Oh! The crowds! The story of their credulity will never end.

DANIEL: For my part, I heard tell—

JOEL: You've all heard tell. As for me, I've seen—

CAIAPHAS: Joel! What have you seen, Joel? You seem troubled.

JOEL: Caiaphas, you would be, if you had seen what my eyes have seen. It's of this Galilean that you were speaking, right?

ANNAS: Yes. Of the carpenter from Nazareth.

JOEL: I am going to tell you very simply what I saw, not dreaming, but awake; if we are awake when we go about and talk, if we are awake here at this moment; and I didn't sleep from the moment of this vision that I had and this moment speaking to you.

ANNAS: You are expressing yourself strangely, brother.

JOEL: Annas, listen to me. It's difficult to express the inexpressible. Which of you doctors knew my cousin, Lazarus of Bethany?

SEMEIAS: Who died recently? I did, Joel.

ANOTHER: And I.

JOEL: If you would like to come with me tonight, or tomorrow to Bethany, Semeias, and you, who knew Lazarus, you will see him living.

SEMEIAS: What are you saying?

CAIAPHAS: Joel, you're dreaming!

JOEL: Answer me! Am I alive?

CAIAPHAS: Certainly.

JOEL: Well then, I am not dreaming, Caiaphas; I am as clean of spirit as you all.

ANNAS: Unfortunately, we are not all.

JOEL: Are you, Annas?

ANNAS: Every man has moments of distraction. I guarantee you healthy and lucid and I consecrate this moment to hear you. Go on, speak. Don't you see the point to which you've aroused our curiosity?

JOEL: It's despite myself that I am speaking. Yesterday evening I was in Bethany trying to console Martha, my cousin, that I had with other relatives accompanied to the sepulcher of her brother. A man came, the same one you were speaking of when I entered this hall.

CAIAPHAS: Ah! The Galilean.

JOEL: Some disciples followed him. Poor folk, who, it appeared had forsaken wealth and family to attach themselves to his person. An Iscariot among others. Mary, Martha's sister, a poor creature, escorted the Galilean. Like you, I knew him by reputation, like you, my brothers, I scorned him.

ANNAS: He was then an acquaintance of your cousin Lazarus?

JOEL: They told me they were bound in friendship.

CAIAPHAS: You are not going to pretend—

JOEL: I'm not going to pretend anything. I'm recounting. I observed this Jesus and, at first, I blushed for the conduct of these two sisters, my cousins. Because Martha prostrated herself before him and called him. "Master," and Mary went on repeating with inexhaustible tears, "If only you had come, he would not have died." He was motionless and mutely looked at the sepulcher. The rest of us, the witnesses were observing silence— terrifying! And he, mute, looked at the sepulcher. And as for me, keeping my eyes riveted on his face, I suddenly saw his eyes heavy with two tears, which were not followed by other tears, two tears which rolled down his pale cheeks and which he did not wipe dry. And he said, "Raise the stone." I heard someone reply, "It's been three days since he was there; he must be stinking." The man repeated, "Raise the stone!" And the stone was raised. The tomb was yawning, black. Without any gesture but in a firm voice, he uttered, "Lazarus, come!" My eyes leapt from my head. Something white was moving in the crevice of the rock, and the cadaver appeared in the opening standing in his shroud, all rigid in his bandages.

ALL: Ah!

JOEL: The man said, "Unwrap him and let him go." The bandages were cut; we saw the living face, the eyes open, blinking; and there he was standing before us and coming towards us. And his sisters and his disciples were prostrated before the one who was looking at heaven. My knees were shaking and I heard the chattering teeth of someone near me, the Iscariot!

DANIEL: Insanity!

SARAI: There are some strange slumbers.

SEMEIAS: He's telling us a dream.

NICODEMUS: He comes from God.

JOSEPH: I believe he is the Messiah.

ANNAS: Joel, return to Bethany; you won't see Lazarus. You had a vision.

CAIAPHAS: First of all, return home and get some rest; then go to the home of your cousins. You will see nothing has changed in Bethany.

JOEL: I saw. Others saw. You can have Lazarus summoned.

CAIAPHAS: So be it. Then he was sleeping.

JOEL: You can sleep for three days?

PHAROS: There are insects whose bite—

NICODEMUS: But which of us would have dreamed that a man buried for three days was only asleep and could be awakened at the command of an ignorant man such as this Galilean who is not a healer so far as I know.

ANNAS: Now there's our other dreamer!

PHAROS: Coincidence!

ANOTHER: One thing is certain: one cannot revive the dead.

DANIEL: No man can revive the dead.

JOSEPH: Eli and the child of the widow of Sarepthah.

NICODEMUS: Elisea and the son of the Sunamite.

DANIEL: Prophets! Men of Jehovah! And who begged Jehovah saying, "O God, won't you return life to this child?"

SARAI: While this one, in an imperious voice and without praying to Jehovah, commanded Lazarus to arise.

ANNAS: That is precisely insufferable. This Galilean is conniving with the spirit of evil.

NICODEMUS: The Galilean would reply to you, "Does the spirit of evil sometimes do good?"

CAIAPHAS: Nicodemus, evil dresses sometimes in the appearance of good. There are beautiful flowers whose perfume kills; and beautiful fruits whose flesh is poison. I say to you that this man must die, in whom Satan is contriving the destruction of Israel; and he will die, I repeat, because it is better one man die than an entire people.

JOSEPH: But if this man is possessed, let's at least try to exorcise him.

A PHARISEE: There's only one efficacious exorcism. A good cross!

DANIEL: How can you speak of exorcising a seditious person who is shouting everywhere, "Pharisees, race of vipers and whitened sepulchers!"

SARAI: Let him die!

ANNAS: Pilate is only awaiting an opportunity to act. By delivering to him this demagogue we will furnish an indubitable proof of our loyalty and our good will.

CAIAPHAS: As the witnessing of Joel must be accepted, this resurrection is an unexceptionable sign of the power conferred on this man by the Evil Spirit. As soon as the rumor of it spreads among the people, there will be only one voice to proclaim him king. And at the same time unleashing on us the Roman eagles.

NICODEMUS: And if he were the king?

ANNAS: Let him come to have his title examined.

CAIAPHAS: And his genealogy.

DANIEL: And his knowledge.

SEMEIAS: Let's not waste time.

SARAI: They are very late. We allowed his fangs to grow and we smiled too much at his audacity while we were arguing with the Sadducees. The people lost interest in our scholastic debates for whom they lack charm and coalesced around this maker of prodigies.

PHARO: Not the people! The scum!

ANNAS: Yet another resurrection like that of Lazarus and Israel will be all scum!

SEMEIAS: It's got to be stopped.

CAIAPHAS: Are we unanimous?

ALL: Let him die!

(Enter Selomith.)

ANNAS: Selomith! What is it?

SELOMITH: There's a man at the door who insists on entering. "I have to see the high-priest," he says obstinately. He pretends to give you the means of seizing the Galilean.

CAIAPHAS: And you kept him at the door? O Selomith, be bold, lead this man in!

(Exit Selomith.)

JOEL: O baseness! O mystery of rogues!

ANNAS: What's wrong, Joel? And with whom are you angry?

JOEL: If this is the man who I think—(enter Judas with Selomith) It's him, the Iscariot! What are you coming here to do, purulence?

CAIAPHAS: Joel, it's up to me to question him.

JOEL: I blush to be a man and the brother of this sick beast.

SELOMITH: Here's the man!

CAIAPHAS: That's fine. Go and don't let us be disturbed. Come forward.

(Exit Selomith.)

ANNAS: Now there's a corrupt face. A diseased beast; that's well said.

CAIAPHAS: Who are you?

JUDAS: Judas Iscariot.

DANIEL: An Edomite.

ANNAS: Long live Edom, if Edom gets us out of our trouble.

CAIAPHAS: You wanted to speak to us? Speak.

JUDAS: I can tell you where Jesus the Nazarene can be found tonight.

CAIAPHAS: Well.

JUDAS: I am able to lead soldiers to the place where he can be arrested.

CAIAPHAS: Who told you we wanted to arrest him? (to Annas) The treasury is not rich; I am feigning indifference. (to Judas) What makes you suppose we want to arrest this Jesus?

JUDAS: The soldiers of the Temple on the outer sanctuary just now—

CAIAPHAS: You questioned them?

JUDAS: I heard them.

CAIAPHAS: Aren't you a disciple of this Galilean?

JUDAS: He deceived me, the impostor!

CAIAPHAS: Ah! How?

JUDAS: He's not the Messiah.

CAIAPHAS: You thought him?

JUDAS: Many believed it, who no longer believe it. He said to us this evening while eating the Passover, "When I shall have left you." Can the Messiah die? "Do this in memory of me." Mustn't the Messiah always dwell with us? And he often says, "Woe to you, Jerusalem." Can the Messiah curse Jerusalem?

CAIAPHAS: And may he not be a prophet?

JUDAS: He said, "You will see heaven open over the Son of Man and the Angels descend to surround him." And no one has ever seen angels. And there have never been any except the poor surrounding him; to whom he commends me to give all the money in the common purse. He is generous because he possesses nothing and is much received in their houses, like this Lazarus.

CAIAPHAS: You are shaking? Didn't he revive Lazarus? Answer.

ANNAS: We're not back to that story.

JUDAS: He's the devil!

JOEL: The wretch!

CAIAPHAS: Silence! Judas, you know that if you give up your master, he will die?

JUDAS: Let him die.

CAIAPHAS: You are ferociously disillusioned.

ANNAS: He already sees himself as royal treasurer or grand butler: somebody in Israel.

CAIAPHAS: He's falling from on high.

JUDAS: He has seduced only the wretched and the women.

DANIEL: And what women!

JUDAS: He makes them love him; he says he belongs to no one. When they came to him to announce that his mother and his brothers were coming to see him, he pointed to us, his disciples, saying, "Behold my mother and my brothers." He has no guts. When a rich man asked him for advice he said, "Leave everything, abandon all, and follow me. Poverty saves the soul." Because he is poor and poor folk relinquish their bread to him and share their bread with him. And who gave him rights over the dead? Lazarus was sleeping contentedly. Will a man ever be sure of sleeping in peace? He's a tyrant. He knows quite well he must die; he knows it. Then why did he come? To preach the impossible? For one must be mad to undo oneself and ruin one's children; and one cannot love everybody, nor return good for evil, nor protect a woman who misbehaves, nor, struck on the right cheek offer the left. And earth is made for man to enjoy, and woman for man to enjoy, and riches for man to enjoy, and one cannot tear out one's heart, nor tear all desire from one's heart, nor close one's eyes to everything. And he says the kingdom is not of this world and that Jerusalem is not the true Jerusalem! The impostor!

PHAROS: These then are his doctrines!

SEMEIAS: A variety of Essenism.

SARAI: Nothing astonishing that the rabble delight in him.

JUDAS: Give me soldiers. Tonight I will give him up to you.

CAIAPHAS: Well, you will have them.

JUDAS: But I want my wages.

CAIAPHAS: What?

JUDAS: The price of blood.

CAIAPHAS: He hasn't been condemned; we will hear him first.

JUDAS: Well, summon him then! Arrest him yourself.

ANNAS: Insolent.

JOEL: Abominable traitor.

CAIAPHAS: It's essential that he be judged this very night.

JUDAS: I want fifty shekels.

ANNAS: Bandit! You are killing us!

JUDAS: I can continue to follow him; I will eat every day at the table of his dupes.

CAIAPHAS: The service is insignificant. You will have twenty shekels. The Temple is not rich. Be Jewish from conscience.

JUDAS: I am an Iscariot. Give me forty shekels. In two hours he will be in the hands of your soldiers. The skin of the worst of wretches is indeed worth forty shekels.

CAIAPHAS: By giving him up you are only doing your duty as an honest man. You will have twenty shekels.

Rehabilitation cannot be bought; don't you have any conscience?

JUDAS: Leave my conscience out of it. Poorer men than you give us greater alms. I've seen a woman anoint his feet with balm worth triple what you are giving me. I want thirty pieces of silver.

ANNAS: You will have them.

CAIAPHAS: But earn them honestly.

JUDAS: Give me them.

CAIAPHAS: Fifteen before, fifteen after. Phaniel, count him fifteen shekels. (a servant goes out and returns with Selomith) Phaniel, is it counted? Is the Galilean accompanied, Iscariot?

JUDAS: By sheep.

CAIAPHAS: No weapons?

JUDAS: Two or three old swords.

CAIAPHAS: How many soldiers will be necessary?

JUDAS: A dozen if there are only his disciples. Thousands if—

CAIAPHAS: If? Why this reticence?

JUDAS: If God meddles with it.

CAIAPHAS: Damnation! You are mad. Selomith, have someone replace you and take fifteen men. You know Jesus, the Galilean.

SELOMITH: By reputation.

JUDAS: He's the one to whom I will give the kiss of peace. I will explain as we go.

CAIAPHAS: Where is he?

JUDAS: In Gethsemane.

CAIAPHAS: The hill of olives. Fine. Go and be diligent. As for us, we will eat the Passover. Selomith, a word. Keep an eye on your guide. If you don't bring the other, don't allow this one the least chance to escape. I'll make him return the money. Get going. (Judas and Selomith leave) Brothers, I am counting on you so we'll have witnesses. Joel, will we have your revived man? In four hours you can go to Bethany and be back. You have good mules.

JOEL: I will bring him.

ANNAS: If you find him alive, of course.

SARAI: Ah! Ah! If not, let him sleep in peace.

(All leave except Nicodemus and Joseph.)

NICODEMUS: Fatal rush!

JOSEPH: They won't dare. His doctrine is pure.

NICODEMUS: And we are not pure enough to understand it. I've argued with him.

JOSEPH: You?

NICODEMUS: Once. Shortly after the death of John the Baptist. A word from him among others struck me. "No one, who is not born again can see the kingdom of God. Flesh is flesh; what is born from the spirit is spirit. The wind blows when it wishes; you hear its voice and you don't know where it is coming from, nor where it is going. Thus it is with someone born of the spirit." I remember, I remember, and since then I haven't stopped thinking of his words, and now, listening to this Judas, I think I understand. Come Joseph, we must talk. I have I don't know what confused notions in my soul. I am extraordinarily troubled. Let's go to my home, if you like. You will be my guest tonight. We won't allow a prophet to be murdered, right?

JOSEPH: Prophet or not: the cruelty of condemning him without sure proofs would be enormous. And I believe him just.

NICODEMUS: He is! He is! More than we. Let's go.

(They leave.)

CURTAIN

ACT II

SCENE 5: THE GARDEN OF OLIVES

JESUS: Keep me company. Let's sit here.

PETER: You are very weary, Lord. Stretch out and sleep a little, while John, James and I, we will watch.

JESUS: It's not the body that is weary, Simon Peter, it's the soul which refuses to sleep.

PETER: Where will we spend the night, Master? Won't we go to Bethany?

JESUS: Should I go to prepare such a mishap for Judas? Those who are looking for me tonight must find me.

JAMES: The Iscariot will betray you, Lord?

JESUS: He will betray me if my father permits it.

JOHN: Lord, wouldn't it be better to hide yourself?

JESUS: Where must one go, John?

JOHN: Out of Judea where they hate you. No one would pursue you in Galilee.

JESUS: Where Antipas reigns, who caused John the Baptist's death. There is no longer any safe place for me any where. Any more than for David fleeing before Saul whom the prophet nonetheless commanded to remain in the kingdom. No prophet has commanded me to remain. My soul alone, and my Father who says, "Don't desert your people, don't abandon the flock I have confided to you." Who to talk to anyway, in the Arabian desert? I belong to this soil and it's not mine to take across the frontier. And as for Galilee, is there one of its towns, one of its cities where I have not planted the seed, one of its Synagogues where I have not unveiled God, one of its ill that I have not cured, one of its wretches that I have not pointed out the way of salvation to? Bethesda, Capernaeum, Corazin, the countryside, the shores of Tiberaide, it's only right up to the great sea and the confines of Syria where I haven't breathed life, combated death and revealed the Spirit. I have nothing more to do in Galilee. I have no more business except in Jerusalem and I cannot avoid it.

JAMES: They wanted to stone you, Master.

PETER: Today again, to arrest you.

JESUS: And, this very night, Judas made a bargain with

the Princes of Priests and the Elders of the people.

PETER: But their plans will be baffled, for you are the Messiah and the Father won't allow them to put a hand on you.

JAMES: And you are in safety everywhere, Master, because the Father protects you everywhere.

JESUS: My soul is sad to death.

PETER: Oh, Lord! The Son of David cannot die.

JESUS: Back, Satan! What do you know of the will of the Father?

JAMES: Master, don't you have words of eternal life?

JESUS: They have not understood me! O John, as for you, did you understand that death is only an appearance?

JOHN: I believe it, Master, without understanding it.

JESUS: Children! Isn't it necessary for the buried seed to rot for the olive to grow? O God, Master, Father, Wisdom, did you will this? Have I sown in the sand? Will I depart having vainly paraded fire and light in these shadowy humans?

PETER: Master, you always speak to us in parables,

which is why we don't understand.

JESUS: Would you understand me if I said: I come from the Father and I must return to the Father having passed through death, and it is necessary for you to do as I have done, that you be tortured as I will be tortured, for you to speak as I have spoken, fearing nothing, no one and that you accept to live and die very bitterly before re-joining me by my Father?

PETER: To die for you, that is very easy, Lord.

JESUS: Very easy? You will have renounced me three times when the cock crows. Easy to die? Yes, when in-deed death has a pretty face—or indeed when coming on wolf's feet it grasps you from behind, with both hands, shutting your eyes, or when it is made to accom-pany glory. I see a different sort of death coming which is not that of a warrior, nor that which leans over the bed of an old geezer, premature death.

JAMES: Lord, you who revived Lazarus, you can give death its dismissal if it comes without your permission: you are its master.

JESUS: Shut up, James, shut up! There's perhaps another obstacle between you and the light beside me. The Mes-siah you comprehend hides from you, perhaps, the veri-table Messiah; my flesh and my bones, O my Father isn't that the trap and the scandal of Israel? Will you make it adopt me when you've taken me away and will you raise up the spirit which justifies the Son of Adam?

PETER: Lord, there are few persons who love you more than I do. You know it, for you see my heart. You know the feeling of each man before he speaks. I cannot believe you would think of leaving us. That would be hard for me and the others, too.

JESUS: Peter, you are speaking like a woman and like a child. Is your faith so weak? Have you lost God, when you lose your brother? And is man ever abandoned when God remains with him? What did I say to you tonight while breaking bread? "Do this in memory of me." Once I've disappeared, have I also disappeared from your mind and your heart? Have I spoken only dead words? Will you forget me as you forget a dream? I did not come to be the friend and companion to Peter, James and John. If it pleases God to break me, I who am his instrument, and to achieve without me the salvation of Israel, is it for us to complain? And will you end by accusing God of it, men of little faith? The love that I am preaching to you is not a carnal love. What are you and what am I? Men, images, shadowy copies of the Eternal Face. And we will go on to love, to give ourselves entirely to one another, brother to brother, wife to spouse, son to father, in accordance with the flesh; man to friend of his choice? What an abyss is between you and me that you don't understand the things I say? What is a friend, a spouse, a father or a brother if not transported by infirm flesh to the titles of the Eternal? There is no other love than the love of the Father! You love me, love me more, it's God that you love in me. Your loves? Vapors of dreams or screams of bestial blood, if you don't know how to discover the love of the Father. You love your wife with ardor and jealousy; and your mother so long as you have need of her protection; your friend because it's nice in life to have a confidant. Let the spouse, the mother and the friend die; if you haven't taken God to witness your loves, of what will you complain if he leaves you in prey to your mourning and if he has no ears for your wailing? I came to tell you this and to show you that a man can do what I say and do what I do without any father but God, and without possessing what makes for pride and the sin of all men, no science, nor concubines, but only certainty that one thing is necessary and not two. To do the will of God, cost what it may, and what ever may be the tremblings of our fragility. If I've made of you men of this faith, if I've been able to prune away your dead wood, to burn your thickets in the fire of this conviction, it matters little to me if I die today rather than tomorrow. You three alone have the ability to speak the language that I am speaking by recreating me in each of your actions in the manner of saying yes or no, in your self denial, in the serenity of your adversity, in the perpetual repetition of the prayer I taught you. "May your name be sanctified; may your reign come, may your will be done!" Nothing except you three and the world. You are no longer listening to me. They are sleeping.

JOHN: I heard you, Lord.

JESUS: What's that noise? Didn't you hear anything?

JOHN: Nothing, Master.

JESUS: Peter, James! Wake up!

PETER: I am not asleep, Master.

JAMES: "One thing alone is necessary—"

JESUS: You can't keep awake a moment with me? Death prowls tonight, and Satan is alert. Let's not let ourselves be surprised. Is this all your friendship? I tell you that my soul is sad to death: will I ask you in vain for the comfort of a prayer?

(He moves away.)

JOHN: Let's pray then.

PETER: Let's pray.

JAMES: For him.

PETER: Let's pray as he taught us. Our Father who is in heaven, may your name be sanctified—

JOHN: May your reign arrive—

JAMES: May your will be done, in heaven and on earth.

PETER: In heaven and on earth.

JOHN: Give us today our daily bread.

JAMES: Our daily bread—

JOHN: Don't let us succumb to temptation.

JESUS: Nothing except a wall of silence and impalpable shadows.

JOHN: But deliver us from evil.

JESUS: No other opposition except hellish carnality. And this silence is unbroken as if I had not spoken; the gauze of shadows, I haven't torn it, I have not been able to impose servitude on the flesh. Who says that? The witness of the carnal eye which sees nothing in the night, and does it see better during the day? The eternal plan is realizing itself unaware that my eyes and my ears do not perceive anything of the march of ceaseless activity; for you are working, O Father, in the silence and the least action of the least creature: a word, a gesture, a breath, the shadow of a thought, has reverberations foreseen by you who wed our destinies to your will. If I've done your will, if I've really understood, if I've served with an exact obedience, if I've placed the cornerstone of the true Jerusalem of salvation, and that you've reserved for those who will follow me to build completely, remove me from the world, O my father! You won't find me rebellious. But at least, if it pleases you, spare me from this bitter chalice of violent death, for I fear weakening and suffering flesh doesn't know any longer what it is saying. All the sadness of the world is in me, motionless, heavy, and I've been unable to shake it off except by seeking your face and you alone know, you alone know. My God! Isn't this enough? So many solitary tears, of nights without name, of days without consolation, all spent dragging the cadaver of human sin. Is that not yet a sufficient example nor a sufficient expiation? What more have I to give? Must I experience in my body all the evil with which my soul was lacerated? If it's possible, my Father, make my death like the death of Elijah and of Moses and let me be spared drinking the bitter dregs of the wine you've made me drink. They are only unfortunate, right? They won't be placed beyond mercy! My God! My Father! If I am your child, don't expose me to such a rough temptation; keep this chalice away from me. I have confidence in you, my Father. They're coming. It's the wind in the leaves. I feel death coming. Father, see my agony. Is it thus that I shall die and will you be content with this sweat of blood? Gethsemane, my tomb? Is it the end? Peter!

(The Disciples approach.)

JESUS: Asleep! Peter! James! And you, too, my John? Can't you watch an hour with me? At this hour even, they are not sleeping. Pray with me that their plans be rendered vain. The enemy never sleeps; we must pray to frustrate his malice.

PETER: We will pray again, Lord, but the night is so calm.

JESUS: Is it calm? Then I hear noises you don't hear? Evil is at work, I tell you! If we see morning, it's to our prayers that we will owe it. And perhaps we will go into Galilee. A few minutes yet, one short prayer again and we will leave.

JAMES: The night is chilly, Lord.

JESUS: Yes, we are going to leave. Yet one more moment, a fervent prayer, and we will leave together, rendering thanks to our father. (he moves off)

PETER: The Master seems to sense a danger. But who will come here to seek us?

JAMES: You have your sword and I have mine. We would die defending him.

JOHN: Let's pray, since he asks us to pray.

JAMES: It's cold. It would be better in a nice bed.

JOHN: Will we be more demanding than he?

PETER: In a few minutes it will go away.

JOHN: Our father who is in heaven—

JAMES: Always the same prayer?

JOHN: It's the one he always says. I'm not tired of it. But it is indeed necessary to meditate on it. One could spend one's life repeating this prayer.

PETER: It's true, John. If all men knew it and recited it every day they would be happier than they are.

JAMES: We are really happy now, John.

JOHN: Why do you say that, James?

JAMES: To think that he is there, he who is the Messiah, the Saviour of Israel and he has chosen us to be the first in his kingdom.

JOHN: If we are worthy of it.

JESUS: And as for me, if I think there is no necessity to die? What benefit would my death be for Israel? Must there be yet another shower of blood so that this sterile people will bear fruit? Then, when my life was so powerless will my death be more efficacious? Wouldn't it be better, appearing in the sun, brandishing a sword forged by your angels and completely armored in gold to descend on Israel at the sound of awakening trumpets of the dead and followed by a sparkling cohort of just men, revived, encircled by a radiant and terrifying guard of angels, to forcefully establish the City of God, the Reign of David that will never end, the imperishable Jerusalem? It's in me to ask you this, my father, it's in you to grant it to me; it requires gold, lightning and glory to dissipate this deafness, to make these blind eyes see. Shall I say the word? Will I be King after having been the pastor? Shall I at last write the first page of divine history? God, do you consent, from tonight, to the resurrection of man? Those torches in the valley. Your response, my Father? It's not the hour of glory, only the hour of death. May your will be done. What is going to follow doesn't concern me any further. I deliver my body into your hands. Ah, at last, action is over, willing is over. Only submission, easy task, an absence of work. (approaching his disciples) Sleep, brothers. But now, I don't have the right to waste a single lamb that the Father has confided to me. Peter, arise! The hour has come.

PETER: To leave, Lord?

JESUS: For us to part. For you to go refit your boat and repair your nets. For me to confront the Pharisees.

JOHN: We won't leave you, Master.

JAMES: Is there some news? Someone has come.

JESUS: Someone is coming. We are encircled by torches. (Judas enters) And here's the one I was expecting.

PETER: The Iscariot! What are you coming here to do, traitor?

JUDAS: Leave me alone.

JAMES: Bandit, you are no longer one of us.

JESUS: Predestination! Who are you seeking, Judas?

JUDAS: You, Master.

JESUS: Greetings. It was you who led them here?

JUDAS: Me?

JESUS: Who are you looking for?

SELOMITH: Jesus of Nazareth.

JESUS: That's me.

PETER: Help me, James. (he strikes a soldier)

SOLDIER: I am wounded.

JESUS: Peter, sword in scabbard. He who strikes with the sword will perish by the sword. If I wanted to be defended I could make a legion of angels shower down, a whole divine army, bustling with lances. Watch me and wait until I say, "Help me!"—Who are you seeking?

SELOMITH: Jesus of Nazareth.

JESUS: That's me.

SELOMITH: In the name of the Sanhedrin, I arrest you. Seize him.

PETER: Lord, command your angels!

JESUS: My Father! The word is burning behind my teeth. Peter, John, James, go away, until God stops them.— Who are you looking for?

SELOMITH: Yourself, if you are Jesus of Nazareth.

JESUS: That's me, I tell you. Is it for me to give myself up? You have come with spears and sticks as if to seize a thief or a murderer. If I were that, would I have waited for you? And if you fear that like Eli the Thesbite, I won't call the fire of heaven on you, the same that consumed the soldiers of Ochosias, of what use do you think your sticks and swords would be? I said a word very low: God alone heard it and you cannot take a single step; if I say another little word the earth will open and bite you! Know God and the one you wish to arrest. And now, seize me; there's no longer a barrier. Do it quickly.

SELOMITH: This is the order of the High Priest.

JESUS: Do it. (the soldiers bind Jesus) But allow them to go.

SELOMITH: I must arrest only Jesus of Nazareth. Let the others go. (the disciples flee) This is the one who denounced you.

JESUS: I know. For how much?

SELOMITH: How much did they give you, man? Answer.

JUDAS: Thirty shekels.

SELOMITH: Yes, I believe it.

JESUS: I know.

SELOMITH: You will easily justify yourself.

JESUS: God knows it.

SELOMITH: As for me, I am only obeying. Come on! March! (they all leave)

JUDAS: That's the way it must end. A little sooner, a little later. That money was still good to take. It's the end of a nightmare. They will return to their boats. In a week the whole world will have forgotten him. Lazarus? Brr! It's cold among the olives. And Magdalene? What to say to her when she learns? I want to tell her. And then as I go to the right or the left with my money I will make interesting friends. But I know what they cling to. I know what it costs to have a disinterested friend. Let's march. And henceforth may this be on all the roads of the world!

(Exit.)

CURTAIN

ACT III

SCENE 6: MARY MAGDALENE

Bethany, in front of the house of Lazarus.

(Enter Cleophas and Nathan.)

CLEOPHAS: This is it.

NATHAN: They must be asleep. Shall we awaken them?

CLEOPHAS: It must be done. They have to know. (he raps)

NATHAN: Sinister messengers, the two of us.

CLEOPHAS: It's less troubling to have to inform a friend than the mother. Peter and John have reserved the most difficult mission. (Lazarus enters) Peace be with you, Lazarus.

LAZARUS: Peace be with you, Cleophas and with you, Nathan. You are welcome.

NATHAN: Don't wish welcome to misfortune.

CLEOPHAS: Speak much lower. Martha and Magdalene will soon enough learn the news. Lazarus, if he wishes will see to informing them.

LAZARUS: I hear you. It's about the Master, isn't it?

NATHAN: Yes, Lazarus.

LAZARUS: Well?

NATHAN: He's been arrested. At this very hour, he's answering his judges.

LAZARUS: Who assumes the right of judging him?

CLEOPHAS: The Sanhedrin, naturally.

LAZARUS: What complaint?

CLEOPHAS: What do I know? Who can know?

NATHAN: How will this end?

CLEOPHAS: With his death.

NATHAN: Cleophas, you think?

CLEOPHAS: From the moment he is only a man like us, and that he is not the Messiah and the King. Who now will be able to save him from their claws, him, the Galilean? We have only to return to our homes and not boast of having known him.

LAZARUS: Cleophas, Nathan, this was your friendship?

NATHAN: We had faith in his word. Why, if he is King, is he allowing himself to be seized like a thief! A sheep without rage. He didn't even show surprise.

LAZARUS: O my Master!

CLEOPHAS: And you are not astonished, either?

LAZARUS: Your astonishment does him injury. You are truly men of little faith.

NATHAN: You who lived in death and live today in life through the will of this man, don't you know any more of him than we know?

LAZARUS: He lives.

CLEOPHAS: In what a poor vacillating life henceforth, which leans towards death and whose good deeds for the living have ceased!

LAZARUS: For him a word suffices to calm the sea, a look to attach it to him. And I can no longer detach myself from him. In the cell, in the tomb, he lives, his word lives and I can no longer hear anything but it amidst the uproar of the world. The word pierced the rock, and death, and my dead flesh and my inert soul. (Judas has come in)

JUDAS: Will you be of an equal help for him?

NATHAN: Judas, what have you learned?

JUDAS: They condemned him. I am coming from Jerusalem. They are going to demand from Pontius Pilate the execution of the sentence.

LAZARUS: You have seen him, him, the Master?

JUDAS: Meeting him as he left the house of Caiaphas, amidst torches. Mistreated by the soldiers, mocked by the servants of the Temple, absolutely treated like the worst of criminals, he made me feel pity. I wouldn't have thought that he could descend to that; that he consented to the infamy of such punishment. If he is innocent, why does he so placidly accept outrage, and if he is the prophesied King, why doesn't he make his bonds snap off? I was ashamed for him and for us. We are besmirched by this derision; despite my pity for him, I wanted to scream: It is well done!

LAZARUS: Cleophas, Nathan, do you permit your ears to hear this?

CLEOPHAS: There's some truth in what he says.

NATHAN: He's ruined our reputation.

JUDAS: And you, Lazarus, he saved you from the tomb only to give his execution one more shameful witness; and to better confound and overwhelm you.

LAZARUS: Do you come from hell? And you were one of his disciples.

JUDAS: Yes, I come from hell, if you mean the hell that travels in his entourage. (to Cleophas and Nathan) You were his only in name, in heart and from a distance. You couldn't know what he made us endure; we who left everything to follow him. You've only heard tell of his cures, of great crowds enchanted with his voice and the tracks of his feet, of our intoxication and exclamations. Hosanna! Son of David! Vain and paltry triumphs which fill these simple souls with joy and courage, my fishermen companions, these souls of mules, that, having once conceived a fable and the vision of the kingdom and the glory, a nothing, the applause of villagers suffices to re-inflame their chimera and to make them forget the weariness, the rebuffs, the sneers of the great; the bleeding feet, the nights of sleet, the burning days. And they delight themselves, these beastly hearts, to caress with their swollen fingers, in a vision, the hot and sweet fleece on the steps of the future throne. We city-folk, we don't have these tenacious rural illusions, right, my friends? You remained prudently at a distance, not neglecting your business, full of a firm and healthy suspicion.

NATHAN: Full of faith and confidence also, Judas, hoping indeed not to die before seeing him on the throne of Israel, gloriously raised above the nations and ridded of Roman legionaries, magnified as in the days of David.

JUDAS: Surely. And as for me, I too had a firm confidence, but each day made a gap and could no longer repair the weight of the feeble purse which was owed to the swollen popular enthusiasm. And it's we who were right and the country-bumpkins now look at themselves confused. Simon Peter, the son of Jonas, and those of Zebedee; they don't understand and they will never understand how their Messiah—ah! ah! ah!—found himself to be one day nothing but a fine rogue, that tonight or tomorrow we are going to watch hang on a cross; and his death will be more profitable to us than his life, if we know how draw profit from the lesson and reverse our judgments.

LAZARUS: It's not possible that the Master did not perceive your spitefulness, Iscariot!

JUDAS: Oh! surely, revived he knows all. He sees spirits, he sounds hearts, but he can't prevent anything.

CLEOPHAS: There's nothing left for us to do but go home.

JUDAS: Nothing more to know. Peace be with you, Lazarus, and with that sister of yours who didn't change her life. You were really good to take back the other one.

Watch her for fear she doesn't commit some new folly with the money she earned at Magdala.

NATHAN: Peace be with you, Lazarus.

(Magdalene enters.)

LAZARUS: Did we awaken you, Mary?

MAGDALENE: No. It's day.

LAZARUS: Already.

MAGDALENE: You didn't sleep tonight, Lazarus.

LAZARUS: Nathan and Cleophas have come.

MAGDALENE: The peace of the Lord be with you, Nathan and Cleophas; and with you, Judas. (greetings) Can I know, brother?

LAZARUS: Awaken your sister, Mary. You and I will go down to Jerusalem. Cleophas and Nathan bring us bad news. The Master has been arrested.

MAGDALENE: The Messiah! Arrested?

JUDAS: The Messiah! What are you babbling to us about the Messiah, poor madwoman!

LAZARUS: Silence, Judas! Don't further scandalize—

JUDAS: The Magdalene scandalized by a word? Yes, woman, Jesus was arrested. And what is more, tried, and what is more, condemned.

MAGDALENE: Condemned! Him! Judas, you are lying, right? You have never inspired me with confidence. Cleophas, Nathan, Lazarus!

LAZARUS: Let's go to Jerusalem. We will know.

JUDAS: Don't go if you are sensible. You will only see lamentable things there. Do you really want to see a man die so much?

MAGDALENE: Die?

NATHAN: The hate of the Sanhedrin is great.

CLEOPHAS: He didn't spare the doctors and the priests in his speeches.

MAGDALENE: You believe that they will kill him?

JUDAS: They will put themselves out to do so.

MAGDALENE: Oh! Let's go! Let's go. All to witness for him. And with us, all the disciples.

JUDAS: Now there's a dangerous madwoman! Compromise ourselves? Us? And for an impostor, a sorcerer? Thanks. As for us we don't push love to that point. Go witness. You, if you wish, with your brother, the resurrected. Perhaps with your see-through dress from Magdala and him with the shroud of the sepulcher, you will make an impression on the tribunal. Or on Pontius Pilate, the Procurator. Witness? Us? On what pretext? On the pretext of dupes. I can hear the laughter when we, morons, will say, "It's we who believed he was king." Let's go, Cleophas, come on, Nathan. I would sooner see you howl with wolves. It's been long enough that we followed the shepherd's crosier of this pastor from hell! He was leading us to the slaughterhouse. Let's be gone; they breathe dementia around this one who returned from the tomb. Rather, let's seek out the company of people of mud and sin; we will find someone to talk to.

CLEOPHAS: I shall return home.

NATHAN: I am returning to my business. Goodbye, Lazarus.

MAGDALENE: Cleophas, Nathan; you aren't going to abandon him like this! Him, the Christ, the King, the Great Friend who loved us so much; you are truly thinking of abandoning him in an hour so dark and bitter?

CLEOPHAS: If he is the Christ?

NATHAN: Yes, why this dark hour?

MAGDALENE: It's a test! It's a test!

NATHAN: A test?

MAGDALENE: Wouldn't a king have the right at the moment of introducing his friends into his kingdom to test their friendship? We pretended to love him. Who knows if this humiliation is not so he can distinguish among us those who love him in truth, and those who love him only with their mouth, their heart being solely occupied with a brilliant greed? Don't you feel remorse or trouble when you speak of returning to your business? You lower your eyes. You see indeed you cannot abandon such a friend in distress. Is there someone other than him? Is there a brother, a relative, a mother you have ever spoken to as he spoke to you? You yourself, Judas, somber heart, I know that all the words you utter against him are returning against you and bite you like serpents. His generosity is more terrible than the wrath of the Eternal One. He who speaks against generosity sharpens the swords which devour him and is preparing for himself a bed of burning coals. Cone on! Let's all go to Jerusalem.

CLEOPHAS: But what can we do for him? As Galileans we will be scorned. Our testimony will not be received. They will stone us if we raise our voice in his favor. The Pharisees won't forgive. What are we?

MAGDALENE: Well, at least we will be there. The Master will recognize us. Indeed, won't you be pleased to have friends at the bed of your last fever, to hide from you the terrible face of death? Indeed, isn't there merit for us to endure some small tortures so as not to leave him all alone amidst the terrors of the day prepared for him.

NATHAN: Well, let's go down to Jerusalem.

JUDAS: I'm not going there. It's not rendering him a service by imposing on him the sight of those he deceived. Your presence will be a reproach to him. An overwhelming reproach. I won't go. I don't like seeing a man die; and this death, were it of my best friend or the worst swindler.

MAGDALENE: Come, Judas, come, too. It's not necessary that he have a traitor amongst the twelve that were dear to him. It's necessary that he see you all.

JUDAS: A traitor? Why do you say a traitor? If there was a traitor amongst us it was him! None other! You don't have the status to judge, to judge me. Who are you to judge me?

MAGDALENE: O Judas, I don't judge you. I am only a wretch who sins, who is remorseful. Don't come if you don't wish to come, Judas.

JUDAS: No, I won't go. If I went there I couldn't prevent myself from shouting, "Christ, you who saved others, save yourself!" And when I shall see him on his cross I fear my furor would exclaim—"Christ, come down from this wood then, you who resurrect others! Maker of prodigies, now is the hour of your prodigies—or never! Triumph! Prove your royalty! Defend yourself or perish!"

MAGDALENE: While he's living, don't defy him, Judas Iscariot.

JUDAS: While he's living? Is he still living? And, if he's living, it's a life so enchained that he'll much prefer to be dead.

MAGDALENE: And who tells you that during the hour of death the hour of glory won't thunder? And aren't you dismayed by being excluded from it, you who lived to possess it? You know quite well he commands death. Look at this one, my brother. You are not dreaming. Here's the sun and he has not vanished. I feel, I know, Oh, I know, I divine! You, today, you dread to hear burst out the very voice which commanded Lazarus to arise. He is living! He is King! He can do what he wishes! At this moment, even when you outrage him, and the sun rises, Jerusalem sees perhaps unheard-of things and echoes with Hosannas!

NATHAN: Let's go; let's all go! Woman, you have restored my faith.

CLEOPHAS: Let's go! For the day won't end without a great miracle having appeared.

JUDAS: They are mad! I tell you, he is bound, condemned. He knows it, he foresaw it. He can do nothing to prevent it! I could tell you—

LAZARUS: Judas, you can only hurt us. You speak from a troubled heart. I pray the Eternal to give you peace. Goodbye, Judas. Mary, we are leaving. Go wake up your sister.

(Magdalene exits.)

JUDAS: I am leaving you. Don't believe that I hate him. But he deceived us. I have difficulty understanding that you take it this way, this reversal, this malice, this—this betrayal. Yes, and that you could still believe in the face of this disaster.

LAZARUS: No disaster. All disaster is for one who doubts.

JUDAS: As for me, I don't doubt. As for you, I could tell you— Perhaps you could understand me.

LAZARUS: I understand you enough to pity you.

JUDAS: No. Ah! Pity me! As for me, I'm safe. As for me, I am bathing in jubilation! It's I who pity you. Resurrected because you are a fool; the sepulcher has rendered you mad. Madness germinates beneath the feet of the Nazarene; it's born from his voice. Life ceases to be angry with itself. It almost makes me mad like you, like your sister who hopes to see impossible things one day.

What then? The heavens open? The angels of Jehovah in the streets of Jerusalem? She won't see anything but a man hanged; about whom no one will speak further tomorrow. And you will be confounded with your madness. Remember what I say to you, me, Judas. And when you are cured, I will tell you to whom you owe your health! Goodbye. We will speak of it again.

(Exit Judas.)

NATHAN: If we are mad, I beg the Lord that he never make me sane like that man.

(The women appear in the doorway.)

CLEOPHAS: Let's go! We are in God's hands.

LAZARUS: Let's go. Life isn't on this side of the tomb.

(Exit all.)

CURTAIN

ACT III

SCENE 7: GOLGOTHA

(Enter Judas.)

JUDAS: He rises and I fall. We didn't have any choice. He was born to be just; I was born to—for what? Nothing. How foolish it is; no one can disobey the demon who receives us as we leave the maternal womb. Jehovah, who created the two of us said, "This one will speak as a prophet and die as a prophet. This one will follow him for a while blindly; and then the scales will fall from his eyes and he will choke in his last sin." David appeared. From the first day of his life, light was his share and fate. And Saul, strong and valiant and handsome as he lived in shadows and died in shadows. Here he is unrecognizable. Him! Scarlet and crowned—with what? The King. I did that! No. There's the Eternal, Jehovah, who knows what he's doing; we are in his hands to execute the decisions of his mind. Yes—Earth! Oh! He's scratching out my eyes. He can't see me bent over like that. He can see nothing blinded by blood. Flee! To be the innocent stones which roll under his feet; innocent! Not to hear the voice which dazzles in my ears, the bitter voice of despair. Strike! Strike him! He's going to fall. Strike! Jehovah is mute. Nothing budges. I will gorge my heart with this vision and let it die in its pleasure.

(He hides in the trees. Enter Jesus, the Centurion and some soldiers. Simon of Cyrene, Magdalene, Veronica, Martha, and other women. John, Nicodemus, Joseph, Daniel, soldiers and servants of the Temple, Cleophas and Nathan.)

CENTURION: Come on! Hurry, man! You aren't moving.

JESUS: Abba! Abba!

CENTURION: March!

JESUS: My Father, have you abandoned me? (fainting) I can't do any more, brother. Pity!

CENTURION: March, I tell you!

JESUS: Pity, brother! This cross is heavy and blood is blinding me. Let me rest a short moment on my hands and knees. I am weak and I think I am going to faint or die!

CENTURION: Up there! Come on, one more effort and we will be there.

A SOLDIER: March! Do you think we are going to carry the King of the Jews on our shoulders?

CENTURION: Let him breathe a minute.

DANIEL: You see! Now behold the one who gave himself out as the Son of Jehovah God! There's the Messiah that you were following! He bleeds like a man and he weeps like a woman.

THE CROWD: Death to the Messiah! The Impostor! The Liar!

CENTURION: They don't love you, your subjects.

JESUS: They don't know what they are doing,

CENTURION: As for you, you know even less. What were you doing to have deserved a promenade like this in the heat, with a hundred pounds on your back and a rest that's awaiting you on the summit? All the same, you don't seem like a bad man to me.

A SOLDIER: A lunatic.

ANOTHER: Who are these women here? Unveil yourselves a little, gorgeous! Do we interest you?

CENTURION: Or the King on all fours! What do you want, my pretty?

VERONICA: I beg you, Lord, allow me to wipe the face of the poor condemned.

CENTURION: He's one of your friends, my child?

VERONICA: Lord, he never did evil to anyone. Indeed, will you—?

CENTURION: Do it, child. It's curious to be hated to this degree by men and loved so grandly by women. Listen to them weep and sob under their veils. You'd say there were no more mothers, or sisters, or mistresses, all these statues of desolation? See how she tenderly wipes the face of this Adonis. By Venus and the Graces, it's touching.

DANIEL: It's a scandal! Make him move, Centurion.

CENTURION: Are you jealous, old man? Calm yourself. Things won't go on much longer. In less than an hour they won't be able to admire him any more, all naked on his wood.

A SOLDIER: Flavius, pass me your gourd. I am dying of thirst.

WOMEN: Ah! Lord! Ah, God! Alas!

JESUS: Women, don't weep for me. Weep for yourselves and for them! The time is near when mothers will envy those whose entrails are sterile. Weep for yourselves, daughters of Jerusalem. For a man who is dying today you will mourn tomorrow for having given day to man. (to Simon) Thanks, brother. Let's go so that everything may be accomplished.

CENTURION: March! Women, get back! You've been warned not to have children!

SOLDIERS: Ah! Ah! Now's the moment to give oneself over, since after us, the end of the world.

(Exeunt Jesus and the Roman soldiers.)

DANIEL: I am returning to the city, Selomith. Be present at the execution of the sentence together with the soldiers and the servants of the Temple. Then come give us an account of the last moments of this rogue and the attitude of the people. For my part, I am edified. Having seen what I've seen I don't have the least doubt as to the justice of the sentence. Nicodemus, Joseph, are you accompanying me?

NICODEMUS: Excuse me, Daniel; however cruel the spectacle may be, I intend to see it. Pilate recognized that this was a just man. I intend to see how the just die.

JOSEPH: It's just not every day a just man dies in Jerusalem.

NICODEMUS: Where ten men die daily.

(They leave in different directions: Nicodemus, Joseph, Daniel and the Jews.)

JOHN: I will follow him. I will have his last look.

CLEOPHAS: And if he was only an impostor?

JOHN: I loved him.

NATHAN: Let's follow him to the end. I no longer believe; I cannot believe.

CLEOPHAS: What, Nathan?

NATHAN: That all powerful Jehovah won't perform a miracle. I cannot believe that Jesus is dying.

CLEOPHAS: Alas, didn't I hear it, that sigh? "Father, have you abandoned me?"

JOHN: All flesh is weak, Cleophas. The flesh sighs but the spirit, the spirit soars.

(Exeunt the women and the disciples.)

MAGDALENE: Martha, will you be as strong?

MARTHA: Unto death!

MAGDALENE: Come then, sister. Lean on my arm.

JUDAS: (entering) Stay, Magdalene; I have a word to say to you.

MAGDALENE: Well, accompany us up there, Judas.

JUDAS: My place isn't up there and I must speak to you. Refuse: I am dying.

MAGDALENE: You have a strange look. Go, Martha, rejoin Veronica. I won't be long, but there is a charitable duty here.

(Exit Martha.)

JUDAS: Why do you want to go up there? It's not a spectacle for your eyes.

MAGDALENE: My eyes have seen so many spectacles that weren't for them.

JUDAS: What's the good of wanting to weep?

MAGDALENE: One doesn't get one's salvation by laughing. Laughter agreed with the frivolous girl of Magdala; it doesn't set with the serving girl of Jesus.

JUDAS: But he's dying. You don't owe him any more service—if you ever did owe him any.

MAGDALENE: Women like us, we don't forget those that we loved. Watch, Eternal One, Our Father, take me from the world the day I shall forget him.

JUDAS: You owe yourself to the living.

MAGDALENE: So long as I will live, and so long as my brother and my Sister live, I will willingly serve them. In the name of Jesus, their friend, they gave me mercy, without any reproach, and they pardoned me as he pardoned me.

JUDAS: They pardoned you! Martha and Lazarus only pardoned you with their mouth; they haven't opened their door to you, keeping their hearts quite shut. And the one who wished to be loved didn't love anybody, didn't give himself to anyone.

MAGDALENE: Judas, he's dying for us.

JUDAS: What?

MAGDALENE: I feel he's dying for us.

JUDAS: Madwoman! He's dying because he didn't know how to cheat death. And at the last moment, when he names his father, Jehovah hasn't aided him. Neither he nor anyone can know the obscure will of Jehovah. The Just and the Unjust go to death by ways unforeseen; if this one had been able to see that his preaching would lead him to Calvary and crucifixion, do you think he would have played the role of the Son of David? He believed in that kingdom and that Jehovah would help him to found his kingdom. Jehovah only wanted to see one more prophet die.

MAGDALENE: Oh! Judas. The cross is up.

JUDAS: Bearing its fruit. Stop and don't look that way. Tell me, if it only required a word to save him, wouldn't you say that word?

MAGDALENE: Oh! Yes! If I were to die of it.

JUDAS: He will die regardless of what you say! And your death won't enable him to walk on earth again. As for me, I said a word to save you. I saw you were in love with a shadow; mad over a dream; lost because of a dream king. And, scorning my soul and the peace of my of my soul, and the peace of my future days and what you name salvation, I said: Let him die! This vision that you see. It's necessary for a human being to tell me, to excuse me, to absolve me.

MAGDALENE: Judas! Unfortunate! Have I really understood you?

JUDAS: Yes. His death is my work. Let's be humble: the work of Jehovah and the Iscariot.

MAGDALENE: O treason! O treason! O treason!

JUDAS: And Jehovah, the author of this treason, of all the other treasons of the Book, and all the deaths of the prophets and the crimes of the kings.

MAGDALENE: You are Cain!

JUDAS: Son of Adam; Son of God! But this one is not Abel. A liar, an impostor who deceived the Israelite people, and again disappointed a grand hope. The Messiah and he's dying? May all those perish who mislead us and lead us to the slaughterhouse! They are great criminals.

MAGDALENE: Your friend! He was your friend!

JUDAS: I know nothing; I don't want to hear anything. The vapor and the scream of blood are filling all the chambers of my skull; my ears are buzzing as if I were drowning. I'm perishing. Save me!

MAGDALENE: May God pardon me; I can only regard you with horror.

JUDAS: He deceived me; I betrayed him.

MAGDALENE: You never loved him.

JUDAS: I don't know how to love. It's not a question of loving in the Law or in the Prophets. I would have been able to obey him if he had commanded. The Ancient Lord of Israel, the All-Powerful, knew how to make himself obeyed. As for me, I am a Jew, not a Samaritan, not a Galilean with a tender heart. A Jew with a hard skull and a rough neck. You've got to speak to me in thunder claps. They promised us Canaan and we forced the frontiers at the point of the sword. The Eternal kept all his promises; there's only one left. We must rule all the nations with a Messiah; a king is owed us. That's promised. The Eternal cannot perjure himself. How can I pardon this Galilean who has only multiplied prodigies the better to deceive us? I cannot pardon; I don't know how to love. The Law commands an eye for an eye and a tooth for a tooth. This one makes us offer the left cheek after the right cheek is smitten. He contradicts the Law. To annul the Law you must be above the Law. He is submitting to it at this hour. He was not the Messiah. Jehovah, The Eternal, doesn't know him. Indeed, I don't know how he was able to seduce so many poor folks. But he speaks as if he were the truth. But it's a voice too sweet for my ears. I tell you for me he needs to thunder, and the column of flame and the pillar of fog must be visible. Woman, I haven't betrayed. It was something which outstrips me. I could only obey. Woman, why don't you understand me? I could love you, yes, you, despite your pale mouth and the starry wrinkles in the corners of your eyes, and your fat body, certain that I could possess an object of desire, a living reality. I cannot love him because he only awakened in me an impossible desire, for a perfection, for a purity, for a triumph that isn't inclined toward my spirit, that my hands cannot and never will be able to grasp. Thinking of it, this drives me mad. I cling to the earth by my entrails. Woman, woman I confess my crime. I killed him. I don't know why. Don't flee me scornfully or I will die.

MAGDALENE: Come with me up there. Come ask pardon of him, from him.

JUDAS: He's only a man! I don't care about his pardon. His pardon would be a shower of fire to me. But me, you have sinned; understand my sin.

MAGDALENE: Come up there.

JUDAS: No.

MAGDALENE: Goodbye.

JUDAS: Magdalene.

MAGDALENE: Jesus! I'm coming. Away from me! Don't touch me, accursed!

(Exit Magdalene.)

JUDAS: Repulsed! By the worst of men, by the worst of women. Down! Down! Soil, absorb me! Shadows, engulf me! Death, you, you alone, final wish. Oh! This intolerable light, the grasshoppers. Cursed be my father and my mother, and you, Jehovah! And you, Galilean! And the priests and Israel! And myself. This money, let them take it back. Yuck! No need for money to purchase death. A rope, a ruined tree. I vomit life, I vomit myself. The Sun (the stages darkens to shadows) is dead! May God be cursed! May the world be cursed!

CONFUSED VOICES: Ah! Ah! Ah! Ah!

JUDAS: More nothing! Emptiness! There's no more of anything. I am the last man living among ghosts. Let me find a tree. Let me return this money.

CONFUSED VOICES: Ah! ah! ah! ah!

BLACKOUT

ACT III

SCENE 8: THE PILGRIMS

(The shadows slowly dissipate. The hall of an inn can be seen. A door open on the twilight. Cleophas, Nathan and a stranger enter.)

CLEOPHAS: No, Emmanuel, dear traveling companion, don't leave us. We will sup together and we will spend the night in this inn.

NATHAN: We were full of trouble and sadness since Jerusalem. Your words have strangely comforted us. But doubts remain in my mind.

STRANGER: What?

NATHAN: You've shown us that all these events had to come about; that all we witnessed in Jerusalem was announced by the prophets, and that Jesus was indeed the Messiah expected by Israel. But how will Israel be saved by this long foretold death?

CLEOPHAS: We the living, will we see in our own time the idols beaten down as predicted by Ezekiel? And will we see Jesus reign over the Jews and the Gentiles as King David announced?

NATHAN: And is it true as Magdalene and Peter found his sepulcher empty, that we will see Jesus resurrected?

STRANGER: Men of little faith, wasn't it necessary that the Christ die the least honorable death so that you, his disciples and all those you will convert may no longer fear those who will persecute you. Because the most relentless enemy, if he can do everything to the body can do nothing to the soul. They can nail flesh to wood, but how will they murder the teaching, if the crucified flesh doesn't consent to blaspheme the spirit? Did the one of whose death you told me renounce life, blaspheme the spirit and curse his doctrine?

CLEOPHAS: He said only, "Everything is consummated."

STRANGER: No renunciation then. You must imitate him to that degree, You must communicate to your brothers the words of life, the secret of immortality. If you are still afraid, after having seen him die; if possessing the truth, you refuse to spread it, to divulge it, you will not be worthy to be called disciples even were it made the price of your repose, of great sufferings, of universal hate and all of your blood. And you won't be of the numbers of the elect of your kingdom. Know him! Elected for all the glory, you are elected for all the sorrow of the world. The world will never pay you for your works. Your task is to resurrect this Jesus in your faithful heart, first of all in your wounds and in your tears and in your teachings, and in your death. Thereafter, vanquishers of the sepulcher to stir it up, imperishable, among the immense conflagration of souls illuminated by your hands from the flame that he himself ignited in your hearts. Make of the world a burning coal of inextinguishable light, where men, on an immense altar no longer sacrifice animals of the old Law, but the inner idols, those of the flesh and the intelligence and the three great luxuries. As for me, I too have seen the horrifying and prodigious misery of mortal man; and seeing it, I measured Satan. And if your testimony is true of the life, actions, and death of Jesus of Nazareth, I tell you that Death and Satan are overthrown; that the salvation of man has come. A man had to come, who, by lowering himself over the abyss, who by experiencing all the evil, all the poverty, all the sorrow of life, a man that Satan tested in his flesh, in his heart, in his intelligence, a man who dared to struggle with all the temptations of the world, by drinking the chalice to the dregs, by draining all the bitterness of death, by sounding even to vertigo all the infirmities of man, by weeping when confronting childhood misery, and its poor love which is an admission of distress, lame manhood, black and despairing, and all the terrible powerlessness, and all the terrible and ridiculous pride of this chaos and this vanity, the human man! He appeared, according to your testimony, and said, "Man is nothing, God is everything, and between Man and God, I will be the intermediary." And he named God "Our Father" and untangled the confused skein of our destinies. He rediscovered the thread and twine of life which reunites man to God, and through which Life, the air, the light, nourishment are communicated to the shadowy child. Nothing lives in man; everything lives in God. And all will pass except this word; heaven and earth will pass and this word will not pass. Recognize this and you will live; your feet are still in darkness but your face is bathing in light. And this Jesus who was made all man, and did not succumb to the shame of being a man, and knew how to find God again, it seems to me that you would be able, by his very living, even in the phantom of his person and his mortal features to discern the face of the Eternal, who made man and this man in particular according to the Eternal plan and who won't drag the human race through the mud only to return to the mud. O disciples, didn't he say to you, watching his death, he had broken the bread thus, that he blessed it thus, and that he had given to those who shared it a supreme meal?

CLEOPHAS AND NATHAN: Lord!

(The Stranger vanishes.)

CLEOPHAS AND NATHAN: Him! It was him! Disappeared.

NATHAN: O Cleophas! My heart burned hearing him.

CLEOPHAS: Joy! Joy! He's resurrected.

NATHAN: Christ is resurrected! O Cleophas! Say it! Say it! Speak! Sing!

CLEOPHAS: And if he had to die—

NATHAN: There is no more death! There is life, my brother.

CLEOPHAS: Love! Truth! There's God!

NATHAN: And all men, all the millions of men that must be led to God.

CLEOPHAS: To joy. O blind men that we were.

NATHAN: I see now! Brother, it's necessary that all our brothers know the news.

CLEOPHAS: And if they crucify us—?

NATHAN: We will be imitating him to that point.

CLEOPHAS: What does death matter?

NATHAN: What does life matter?

CLEOPHAS: There's an eternal life.

NATHAN: Which doesn't know death! Where Christ

reigns.

CLEOPHAS: Where Christ reigns!

CURTAIN

ABOUT FRANK J. MORLOCK

FRANK J. MORLOCK has written and translated many plays since retiring from the legal profession in 1992. His translations have also appeared on Project Gutenberg, the Alexandre Dumas Père web page, Literature in the Age of Napoléon, Infinite Artistries.com, and Munsey's (formerly Blackmask). In 2006 he received an award from the North American Jules Verne Society for his translations of Verne's plays. He lives and works in México.

www.ingramcontent.com/pod-product-compliance
Lightning Source LLC
LaVergne TN
LVHW091306080426
835510LV00007B/390